The
PICTURE-PERFECT
GOLF SWING

The
PICTURE-PERFECT
GOLF SWING

The Complete Guide to
Golf Swing Video Analysis

MICHAEL BREED ·
WITH GREG MIDLAND

ATRIA BOOKS   New York • London • Toronto • Sydney

ATRIA BOOKS

A Division of Simon & Schuster, Inc.
1230 Avenue of the Americas
New York, NY 10020

First Atria Books trade paperback edition May 2008

ATRIA BOOKS and colophon are trademarks
of Simon & Schuster, Inc.

For information about special discounts for bulk purchases,
please contact Simon & Schuster Special Sales at 1-800-456-6798
or business@simonandschuster.com.

Designed by Dana Sloan
Photographs by Sam Greenwood

Manufactured in the United States of America

10 9 8 7 6 5 4 3 2 1

Library of Congress Cataloging-in-Publication Data

Breed, Michael.
    The picture-perfect golf swing : the complete guide to golf swing video
analysis / by Michael Breed with Greg Midland.—1st Atria Books
trade pbk. ed.
        p. cm.— (Atria nonfiction original trade)
        1. Swing (Golf) 2. Golf—Training. I. Midland, Greg. II. Title.

    GV979.S9B75 2008
    796.352—dc22

                                        2008003436

ISBN-13: 978-0-7432-9027-2
ISBN-10:   0-7432-9027-5

To my father, William C. Breed III, who was the greatest teacher to impact my life. We only get one, and I got the best. May you rest in peace, Pop.

CONTENTS

# Introduction

Why would someone write another golf instruction book? I mean, is golf really in need of another one? *You bet!!* Thousands of instruction books have been written during the evolution of the game, and you most likely have a couple in your bookcase. So why is this book different?

The answer is simple: the video camera. Using a video camera is the only way that you can truly self-diagnose your swing flaws. Other instruction books offer very useful material, but the problem is that what you are told to do and what you are doing are not the same, despite what you think. The video camera is the bridge between what you feel and what is real. This book will be a manual that teaches you to use the video camera correctly and effectively. I'm going to explain to you how to buy the camera, how to position the camera, how to use the camera properly, and most important, how to know what the video camera is telling you. You will learn about cause and effect. You will begin to understand why your golf ball goes in a certain direction. The video camera is the key, given the proper explanation of how to use it and how to interpret the images of your swing. It will unlock the secret to the golf swing in general and, most important, your own individual golf swing.

To get the most out of this book, you must believe this: anyone can play the game of golf. You don't have to be the best athlete to play well, and you can easily help yourself if you have a basic understanding of what you should be doing during the swing. I've amassed my knowledge through hard work and by learning from my mentors and peers. I've spent time trying to understand the golf swing and learning how to explain it to my students in a way that makes sense and is easy to comprehend. You can gain that same knowledge if you take the time to understand what's being presented in this book.

This book will explain the golf swing in a manner completely different from what you're used to. It will make sense! You will learn the reasons behind the changes that you need to make to improve your golf swing. I've always taught the game to my students with the goal of furthering their understanding through logic. The golf swing is not hard to understand; it's the language that instructors use that confuses us.

I chose to name this book *The Picture-Perfect Golf Swing* for a number of reasons. The primary reason is that there is one major problem with learning the game by yourself: in the golf swing, what you *think* you are doing is not always what you *are* doing. There is a common phrase used among teachers; we tell our students, "What you feel is not real." That means that when you are by yourself and doing something such as swinging the club back on plane, even though the swing feels right, you may not be doing it correctly at all. This is such a foreign concept. You have a connection between your brain and your body, but in the golf swing, that connection is often flawed.

This disconnect is the primary reason I initially had a tough time as a young instructor. I was having trouble getting through to my students. On many occasions, I would tell a student to make a certain adjustment. They would do what they felt was correct, but it would not be what I wanted. Yet they would insist they were doing it the proper way. When I would tell them they were not, we would be at an impasse.

They did not improve and would stop taking lessons, and I found I had no business.

When I bought my first video camera and began using it to help me work on my golf swing, I was stunned to see that what I thought my swing looked like was nothing close to what it actually looked like. The reason is that disconnect between what I felt I was doing and what I was actually doing. This was a staggering revelation. I'm a strong athlete, and I've always been able to perform any physical action that I desire. And it dawned on me at that point that my students must be having the same problem. I had to show my students what their swings looked like and explain what they were supposed to look like. I needed to make sure they understood that the video camera was not lying to them. Even though they thought they were performing a certain move, it was not occurring. The advantage of the camera was instantaneous feedback, allowing my students to pursue the correct swing changes. Another positive was that I, as the teacher, was no longer seen as incorrect. An immediate trust was created by using the video camera. My students were able to see what I was attempting to fix, and when we worked on the change, I could show them exactly what they were doing wrong. If a student needed to exaggerate their swing in order to get it right, the video showed just that. Teaching became much easier, and learning was taken to a new level.

It is my belief that video technology is the primary reason the golf swing has evolved considerably in recent years. Golf swings are beginning to look more and more alike, and fundamentals are more consistent from player to player. There is no doubt that the advances in game-enhancing golf clubs have allowed average amateurs to play better golf, but the use of the video camera has taken the game to a whole new level.

In addition to the video camera, I suggest getting a full-length mirror if you don't already have one. This basic yet extremely valuable item will assist you when you're unable to use your video camera. It will also help you make progress on your own when you're unable to get outside. A simple way to improve your game is to continue to work on parts of it during off times, like winter or inclement weather. If you place a golf club next to the mirror, it will encourage you to practice and work on things like posture and ball position, and it will invite you to hold a golf club when you might not otherwise.

The video camera and the mirror are necessary to achieve the main objective of this book: to make you a better player and give you the knowledge to fix your own swing. If you understand the reasons for changing your swing and how to make the change, you can work toward your goal of playing consistently good golf. In addition, understanding cause and effect in the golf swing will enable you to know what is really going on in your swing, rather than guess. Armed with that understanding, you will be well on your way to becoming the player you want to be.

The
PICTURE-PERFECT
GOLF SWING

CHAPTER ONE

The Camera

The purpose of this book is to teach you to teach yourself a better golf swing using the video camera. If you're going to teach yourself how to swing the golf club properly, you must learn how to use this tool properly.

I've spent much time learning how a certain camera or camera angle affects the appearance of a golf swing. In short, you must be consistent about where you position the camera in order to be consistent in your analysis of your swing. In this book, I will arm you with information I have amassed over twenty years of golf instruction. I suggest that you read and reread this chapter until you fully understand how to position the camera. Do that, and you will have at your disposal the tool that, more than any other, has helped instructors improve their students' golf swings.

Not only is the positioning of the camera important, but so is the camera itself. A number of factors affect a camera's suitability for analyzing a golf swing, and I will discuss these later in the book.

The two primary angles you'll be using to record your swing are "down the line" and "face-on." For a down-the-line angle, the camera is positioned behind the ball so that the camera is looking at the right side of your body and toward the target (**PHOTO 1**). For a face-on angle, the camera is positioned directly in front of your chest, so your shoulders and hips are perpendicular to the camera (**PHOTO 2**). These two camera angles will offer you the most assistance when you're analyzing your swing. I use these two angles exclusively in over 95 percent of the lessons I give. All of the information you will need can be derived from these two angles.

Now I will show you how to position the camera for each angle—specifically, I'll explain why the height of the camera is important and why it should be the same from both angles, regardless of what club you're using. It's not a bad idea to use masking tape or chalk on the legs of your camera tripod so you can more easily remember how to set up your camera each and every time.

DOWN-THE-LINE CAMERA VIEW (**PHOTOS 3–13**)

It is critical that you position the camera correctly in order to gain accurate feedback. In the down-the-line angle, there are three important measurements to remember: 1) the distance between the camera and the ball; 2) the distance between the camera and your target line; and 3) the camera's distance from the ground. If any of these positions is incorrect, the images of your golf swing will be distorted, leaving you with incorrect information. Further, you must position the camera consistently from session to session in order to monitor your progress (and be sure you're comparing apples to apples!). So once you have the camera set where it should be, it's a good idea to write down how far it is from the ball, where it is in relation to your target line, and how high off the ground it is, so you can remember for the next time. After you have had some experience positioning the video camera, setting it up properly will become easy.

Let's start with the camera's distance from the golf ball. It will depend a little on the camera itself, but as a rule, the distance should be about twenty feet. Just remember that your goal is to make sure you can see the complete arc of your swing. You don't want to get so far away that you can't see the clubface angle at the top, and you don't want to be so close that the clubhead swings out of the frame at various positions.

Look at the eleven-frame swing that begins with photo 3. As you can see, the camera is able to pick up the complete path of the club and, most important, the angle of the clubface at the top of the swing. The purpose of the video camera is to allow you to correct any flaws in your swing. If you are unable to see the clubface during the entire swing, you might not be able to identify what you need to address to improve your swing. Again, experience will be your best friend.

Now that you have found the correct distance from the ball, let's determine the line on which you should set the camera—that is, the point to which the camera should be perpendicular. There are four common

lines used in video golf instruction for the down-the-line angle; the first three are the ball line (**PHOTO 14**), the toe line (**PHOTO 15**), and the hand line (**PHOTO 16**). But I recommend that you set the camera on the fourth line, which is between the ball line and the hand line (**PHOTO 17**). This point will vary with each club, but as a rule it will be where the end of the grip meets the club shaft.

You can see how different the address position looks in these various camera angles. The two that differ the most are the ball line and the toe line. When you examine the ball line angle, you will notice that there appears to be a large amount of the left side of the body visible. This angle might give the impression that I am set up closed to the target. Now compare this to the toe line angle, and things change dramatically. You are unable to see the left side of the body. In fact,

other than the left foot and the left hand, no part of the left side of the body is visible. I am set up the same way and aiming at the same target, yet the address position looks very different in this angle. This is why it is so important to be consistent in your positioning of the video camera.

Looking at the camera screen, you should see the same amount of space to the right of the golf ball as there is to the left of the rear end. This position will allow the greatest amount of information to be captured by one camera angle.

Determining the height of the camera is quite simple. I suggest you position the camera so that the center of the lens is at the height of your waist. The reason is that one of the most important positions in the swing is when the club shaft is parallel to the ground, which should occur on the

backswing when your hands are around thigh- to waist-high (**PHOTO 18**). Because the camera will not change height during the swing, it must be in a location that allows it to capture all parts of the swing, including this critical position, and centering it on your waist will achieve this. First take a tape measure and record how many inches your belt buckle is above the ground when you are in your golf posture. Then place the camera on a tripod and measure from the middle of the lens down to the ground. The middle of the lens should be at the height of your belt buckle when you are in your golf posture. If you are hitting on a range mat, remember to allow for the height of the mat in order to be consistent.

Another thing to monitor when positioning the camera is the amount of space visible at the top and bottom of the frame. There should be only a little bit of space between the bottom of the frame and your feet (**PHOTO 19**). This will allow for the maximum amount of space at the top of the frame. Remember, you always want to see the entire movement of the clubhead throughout the swing, and if the camera is positioned poorly, you will lose the clubhead at crucial moments. When you adhere to these principles of camera positioning, you'll be able to view your swing in its entirety and see exactly what is transpiring throughout the motion.

FACE-ON CAMERA VIEW (**PHOTOS 20–30**)

This angle is the easier of the two to set up, since there are only a few guidelines for positioning the camera. First, it should be mounted on a tripod at waist height. Second, your body should be centered in the frame, so there is equal space in the frame on both the left and right sides of your body. Regardless of the ball position or the club you are using, your body should always be centered in the frame. Therefore, do not position the camera so it lines up with the golf ball. Doing so will produce an image in which many important components of the swing—including ball position, weight transfer, and impact—are distorted. It is essential to always have the camera centered on your stance so you are consistent with your analysis.

The ideal distance from the camera to your stance line is about twenty-five feet, depending on your height, your swing width, and the length of your golf club. Obviously the arc of the clubhead will be greater with a driver than with a sand wedge. Further, the distance will depend a bit on how much you zoom in the camera lens. But if you use twenty-five feet as a starting point, you can usually adjust the lens to widen or tighten the frame for the perfect position. This positioning will allow you to properly film an eleven-frame sequence of your entire swing, from start to finish (photos 20–30).

There should be a small amount of space between the bottom of the frame and the golf ball (**PHOTO 31**). Further, there should be enough space on both the left and right sides so that the clubhead and shaft do not go out of the frame at any point in the swing (**PHOTO 32**).

Finally, the amount of space at the top of the frame should allow you to see the complete motion of the club. When you draw a horizontal line across the frame, it should bisect your body below your left

31

armpit (**PHOTO 33**). This should provide enough space for the whole club to be seen in every frame throughout the swing. As with the setup, it will depend on your height and the club you are swinging, but this is a good baseline to work from. You will get more comfortable with the proper positioning the more you use the video camera.

THE CAMERA

Now we get to the essential element of the book—the video camera itself. I have had many discussions with my fellow instructors about the video cameras we use in our professional lives, and many of us closely follow the technological developments in video cameras that allow us to provide even more information to our students. Cost and effectiveness are the two most important factors to consider when you're purchasing a camera. I tend to pay more attention to effectiveness, because my first priority is what is best for my students. So is a top-of-the-line camera necessary for the work you will do? You will have to answer that question for yourself, but here are some important guidelines.

First, it is important to have a *digital* video camera. While some nondigital video cameras can perform nicely and record the golf swing properly, long-term use of the video camera will require that you go with digital technology. You will likely use the camera for more than just filming your golf swing, and digital is the only way to go. Also, if you plan to load your swings onto your computer, it is best to have a digital video camera. A digital camera is the only kind that will allow you to e-mail images of your golf swing. Last, the image quality of a digital camera is much better and the cost is not that much greater.

I recommend a video camera with an LCD screen. An LCD (liquid crystal display) is a screen that flips open and allows you to see what the camera is recording without having to look into the viewfinder. These screens vary in size from camera to camera, but many of the better models have an LCD screen of about two and a half inches square.

Some cameras have larger LCD screens, and while that may be of some assistance, it will not make that big of a difference. The important thing is that you are able to view your swing without peering into a small viewfinder, and for this the LCD screen is essential.

Another essential is a remote control. Most cameras these days do include a remote, but you should definitely make sure yours does, because you are going to rely on it more than you might think. Be aware of the need for a remote so you do not make a big mistake and spend hundreds of dollars on a video camera that doesn't include one. Some models operate only with a remote, and on others, the remote has additional features (such as slow motion) that aren't accessible on the camera body itself.

Although the advantages of the remote are many, make sure to purchase a camera that allows you to operate all its functions from the camera itself. This dual operability sounds obvious, but in fact it is not always the case. Some companies will attempt to save you money by not offering this option on their cameras. The problem is that if you break, misplace, or lose the remote, you will not be able to operate the camera. If the remote's batteries run out, the practice session will be a waste. Finally, if you leave the remote at the house, you aren't going to be able to operate the camera on the practice tee. I've made some of these mistakes, and I've always regretted being unprepared. In fact, I've purchased additional remotes and additional batteries to avoid potential problems. So I emphasize these two main points: Make sure the camera you buy has a remote, and make sure it can be operated without a remote. And if possible, buy an extra remote just in case.

Another point to look for when you purchase a camera is the ability to advance your swing sequence frame-by-frame. Some cameras or remotes will not allow you to view the video in this way, but this feature is essential for good swing analysis. You must ensure that the camera you purchase allows you to use the remote to view each frame one at a time.

The final important consideration that I want to address is the camera's shutter speed. The shutter speed determines whether you will be able to view a clear image while analyzing each frame of your swing. I won't get too technical in my description of shutter speed, because it will only cause confusion. Ideally, you want the club shaft to be clearly visible when it is in motion during the swing. If you don't have a high enough shutter speed, the camera will not capture the movement of the club shaft clearly, and the image will be blurry. Note that the higher the shutter speed, the more light you will need to record the image of your swing properly.

The minimum shutter speed necessary to capture the golf swing clearly is 1/1,000 second. I most often shoot with a shutter speed of 1/2,000 or 1/3,000. On a bright day, I will use 1/4,000 or possibly even higher, depending on the time of day and how high the sun is. While the highest shutter speed on the cameras I use is 1/10,000, I rarely, if ever, use such a high setting. The important thing is having the ability to change shutter speeds so you can adjust to changes in the amount of daylight.

Lower-priced cameras will often include a "sports mode" shutter speed option. The exact speed of the shutter in this mode varies with each manufacturer. Typically, the sports mode does provide basic clarity of the club shaft during the golf swing, though cameras that allow you to set the shutter speed numerically offer better clarity. The more expensive cameras have a dial that allows you to set the shutter at the exact speed you desire.

When you purchase a camera according to the guidelines above, it will have everything you need to make an honest and helpful evaluation of your swing.

CAMERA ACCESSORIES

I advise you to pay close attention to accessories. First, you should have more than one camera battery with you at all times when you are recording your swing. Even with a very high-end camera, it is a common experience to have the battery die while you are out on the driving range during practice. The average battery that comes with a camera lasts about one hour, and chances are you will be practicing for longer than that (I hope!). You can purchase backup batteries that last about four hours—I take three of these with me on every lesson. Not that I would ever ask a student of mine to practice for twelve straight hours, but having at least two extra batteries with you will ensure that you never run out of power.

Next, I urge you to have a sturdy camera bag to carry everything you'll need out to the practice range, including extra memory cards and tapes. I recommend having at least two cards and three videotapes, and while you won't need that many, having them in your bag will put you in good shape. Also, I would suggest transferring the footage of your swing to tapes and filing them away. They are a record of your progress, and you may find it valuable to go back and refer to them weeks or even months later. I suggest you label the tapes with the date and a short summary of what you're working on in each practice session. This information will help you tremendously when you review your swings.

Another point of emphasis is the camera tripod. Tripods are made with handles on either the right or the left side. I'm right-handed, so I buy tripods with the handle on the right. If you're left-handed, you'll actually have an easier time of it, since most tripods come with the handle on the left. This is because the majority of tripods are made for still cameras rather than video cameras, and it is assumed that the photographer will need his right hand for the shutter release button. Since we're talking about video cameras, you should simply buy a tripod that has handles on your dominant hand's side (right for right-handers, left for left-handers).

One additional tip: You'll need to determine if you want to save swings onto your computer or simply save the tapes and watch them on a monitor. I do both, but I find it easier to compare swings loaded onto a computer. Various video software programs enable you to view and analyze your swing once you've downloaded it to your computer, but I use the V1 program, which is very common among teaching professionals. I believe that the V1 setup is the best on the market for a variety of reasons, most notably its technological advancement and customer support. Finally, the program is very user-friendly. You don't need to be a computer specialist to understand the V1 system. Navigating from swing to swing is very easy, and you will also be able to e-mail swings, which can be very handy if your golf professional is out of the area. You can view their products at www.V1golf.com.

CHAPTER SUMMARY

- The positioning of the camera and the use of the two main angles for recording the swing (face-on and down the line) are crucial to getting helpful information from the video.
- Mark down the positioning of the camera and the tripod so you can consistently return to the exact same height and location.
- Digital video cameras are a necessity and should be purchased with a remote control, a tripod, extra batteries, and extra tapes.

CHAPTER TWO

The Fundamentals of Pre-Swing, Swing, and Practice

As I discuss the various descriptions of pre-swing and swing technique, please know that the references to "left" and "right" as they relate to parts of the body are written from a right-handed perspective. Readers who play left-handed, please remember that a reference to a "right hand" or "right arm" in the book will actually be reversed for you, meaning your left hand or left arm.

THE GRIP

The first step to understanding the golf swing is learning how to hold the club correctly. The manner in which you grip the club will affect your address position. In fact, your grip will affect the entire swing motion. No matter what your physique, age, or ability level may be, there is a correct way to hold the golf club, and there are many ways to hold it incorrectly. The correct grip allows your wrists, arms, and body to move naturally and freely. An improper grip causes tension to build in your hands, forearms, and elbows, leading to poor swing mechanics.

The ideal grip begins with your left hand, and as you go through the following steps, you should continually use the video camera and the mirror to check your grip. You should hold the club so that your left thumb is farther down the shaft than the first knuckle of your left index finger (**PHOTO 34**). The heel pad of the left hand should rest on top of the grip and not to the side. If the knuckle of your index finger is even with or lower than the tip of your left thumb, you are holding the club too much in the palm of your hand. To hinge the club back and swing it through with power, you need to hold the club more in your fingers and less in your palm.

Once you have the correct left-hand position, it is very easy to achieve the proper right-hand position. Because you cup your right hand over the grip, a small pocket forms in the palm of the right hand, and the thumb of your left hand should fit into this pocket (**PHOTO 35**). This is true whether you're using an interlocking, overlapping (as illustrated in the photo), or ten-finger grip. When you do this properly, the pad of your right thumb will rest on top of your left thumb, which should no longer be visible (**PHOTO 36**). One other point to note is that the V's formed by the thumbs and index fingers on both hands should point between your right breast and right shoulder. There is a lot of leeway here because hand size varies from player to player. If you have smaller-than-average hands, the V's will point closer to your right shoulder. Players with larger hands will see the V's point closer to their right breast.

Also, the positions of your two thumbs relative to each other are important. As you look down at the club at address, your left thumb should be on the right side of the shaft, and your right thumb should be on the left side of the shaft (**PHOTO 37**). This will allow the club to lie across your left hand at about a sixty-degree angle (**PHOTO 38**), which is perfect. This indicates you are holding the club more with your fingers than your palm and will allow your wrists to hinge the way they should in the swing.

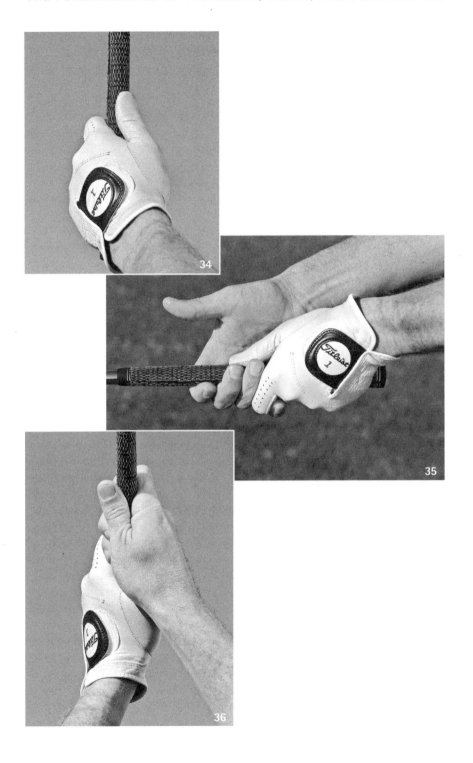

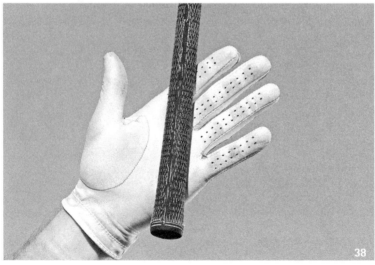

Understand the importance of a good grip, and you will come to understand how to swing the club with minimal effort. The reason is leverage—a proper grip gives you proper leverage, which is crucial in the golf swing because it gives you strength that you might not otherwise have. The root word of leverage is "lever," and every good golfer, no matter what their swing looks like, creates a lever at some point in their swing. In a golf swing, the proper grip provides the proper lever. If you hold the club in such a way as to allow the lever to occur, you have a good chance of making an effortless swing that creates power. If you have a bad grip, you will severely hamper your ability to create leverage and will consequently lose valuable yards. It's just that simple!

The lever is created by your left forearm and the shaft of the club. The angle formed by these is directly related to potential clubhead speed and, ultimately, potential distance. The lever also gives you the ability to swing the club with power while remaining in balance. I will discuss this in more detail later in the book.

Knowing all of this, you can see why it's impossible to overemphasize the importance of a good grip in creating a sound golf swing. Many great instructors have said this through the years, and I thoroughly agree. The proper grip will not make a good swing, but it does allow one to happen. An improper grip, however, will never allow a good swing.

POSTURE

It has been said by many people over the history of golf instruction, and it's true: most of the errors in a golf swing occur well before you move the golf club. By having good posture and the correct address position, you will be able to make a good golf swing.

There are many elements to a proper address position. Here are several key points I will emphasize:

- width of stance
- knee flex
- waist bend
- spine tilt
- arm hang
- shoulder position
- hip position

All of these are related, and poor form in any one area can affect some or all of the others. I will discuss each of these elements and the effect they have on how you stand to the ball.

First, let's look at the width of your stance. This is not only important, but one of the most commonly misunderstood elements of the game. In golf, your weight must transfer from one side to the other, never in an up-and-down fashion. Therefore, it is critical to set your feet wider than your hips at address. No matter what club you are using, your stance must be wider than your hips in order for you to have balance throughout the swing and proper weight distribution. In any motion where weight is transferred laterally—like it is in the golf swing—your feet must be set wider than your hips (**PHOTO 39**). When you attempt to understand the motion of the golf swing, you must understand the role your feet play in creating a stable foundation.

For clues, look at other sports in which weight is also transferred laterally. Watch a baseball shortstop waiting for a ground ball or a tennis player returning a serve. The common link is that the players set their feet wider than their hips. The reason: In order to move their weight laterally, they must push off one foot or the other. They're not trying to move their weight up and down, in which case their feet would be set very narrowly (think of a diver preparing to jump from the diving board or a basketball player shooting a jump shot). When you position your feet inside the width of your hips (**PHOTO 40**), you can control your weight going up and down, but you cannot control it from

side to side. Consequently, a narrow stance will not help you in the golf swing, because it prevents you from making the desired weight shift from side to side.

The next element is knee flex, which is quite simple to understand. Your knees must bend sufficiently to allow for the proper transfer of weight. Think of the example of the baseball shortstop again—in addition to his feet being set wider than his hips, his knees are bent. This is true for all athletic motions, as knee flex allows for your weight to move freely while also helping to maintain your balance. It is nearly impossible to shift your weight without bending your knees—unless you plan on falling over!

The question in golf is: How much knee flex should you have? The answer differs from person to person, but the general response is "only a little." When you bend your knees properly, you should have a slight

flex, so that your knees are over the saddles, or midpoints, of your feet and not your toes (**PHOTO 41**). The variance in the degree of knee flex depends on your height. Shorter players generally require a little less knee bend than taller players, because their spine angle is more upright than it is for taller people, who have to bend over more to reach the ball. (Think of taller players such as Ernie Els, Vijay Singh, and Dan Forsman versus shorter players like Jeff Sluman, Corey Pavin, and Fred Funk.) Your knees should be flexed so that your weight is balanced on your feet at address. You should be able to wiggle your toes at address. If you can't do this easily, you have too much knee flex and you are leaning too far forward as a result. Work on this repeatedly, and you will gain a greater comfort level and a better understanding of the correct degree of knee flex for you. The important thing to remember is that, yes, you must have knee flex! If you stand with your legs locked or too stiff, you'll have a difficult time transferring your weight properly throughout the swing, and your balance will suffer. The video camera

will help you determine the correct amount of knee flex for you and will also help you distribute your weight properly.

Waist bend is extremely important in understanding the correct spine angle. It describes the angle at which you set your upper body in relation to the ball. If you bend incorrectly at address, you will stand at an improper distance from the ball, and your weight distribution will be out of whack.

When you have the proper amount of waist bend, and therefore the proper spine angle, you will notice a couple of things when you view your setup using the video camera from the down-the-line angle. First, your rear end will be about four to six inches past your heels (**PHOTO 42**). You can measure this by holding a golf club against your rear end and letting it hang down toward the ground (**PHOTO 43**). Second, your back and shoulders will appear to be fairly straight and will be at about a forty-degree angle relative to the ground. This is critical, as it allows maximum mobility for your upper torso and shoulders during the swing. If you bend improperly, your back will appear rounded, which greatly inhibits your movement and stiffens your upper arms and body. It also promotes more of an arm swing, thereby limiting body motion and reducing the power you can create at impact. Here are two other indicators that you have too much spine angle:

- You will have trouble wiggling your toes because too much of your weight will be over the front of your feet.
- Your arms will hang down perpendicular to the ground.

Either of these problems will result in a poor motion through the ball, as the club can take a variety of swing paths. This will make it harder for you to square the clubface at impact and hit straight, true shots repeatedly.

So now you know what not to do as far as waist bend and how it relates to spine angle. What should the proper position look like? As discussed before, too much spine angle at address will cause your arms to hang perpendicular to the ground. Your swing will become too vertical, forcing your body to move too much up and down. Your arms should hang at a slight angle toward the ball, so your hands are away from your body and not encroaching on it (**PHOTO 44**). When you are in the correct position, your hands will appear to be on your toe line as you look down at the ball from address (**PHOTO 45**). If they are outside your toe line as you look down at the ball from address, your chest may be too far from the ball. This means you have either too much knee flex or not enough waist bend (**PHOTO 46**). If your hands appear inside your toe line as you look down at the ball from address, then your chest is facing too much toward the ground (**PHOTO 47**). You can correct this with more knee flex or less waist bend, or both. When you have the correct amount of waist bend, your spine angle and the club shaft line will form an angle of around ninety degrees or greater (**PHOTO 48**). As you can see from the picture, my angle is greater because of the length of my arms. In order to accommodate the arm length, my angle will increase.

>90°

Arm hang is critical because it will affect how the golf club returns to the ball at impact. The only way to return the club so that you are "under the ball"—a phrase I will cover in more depth later in the book—is to have your arms hang slightly out from your body at address. Here's why: in order to make powerful contact with the golf ball and hit the shot the way you want to, you must extend your arms through the hitting area. If your arms are perpendicular to the ground at address rather than hanging slightly out, you will bring the club down on top of the golf ball and make a glancing, rather than a direct, strike. This would be a good position if you were trying to hit the ball into the ground, but of course that's not what we're after. So when your arms are set up properly, they should hang away from your body a little bit (**PHOTO 49**), as I described before in the section on waist bend and spine angle. As you move to longer and longer clubs, all the way from

49

a wedge to a driver, your arms should extend slightly farther out. The difference isn't much, but it still has an effect on arm hang and the position of your arms at address.

Another key element of the proper setup is shoulder position. Your shoulder position is related to arm hang and spine tilt. If you set up with your shoulders open to the target line (**PHOTO 50**), your arms will tend to hang too vertically and your spine will tilt toward the target—not the ideal position. Since your right hand is lower on the grip, your right shoulder should be lower than your left shoulder; at address your spine should tilt slightly away from the target. Your shoulders should have a slight upward angle, giving you the proper tilt (**PHOTO 51**). Your left arm should be higher than your right arm, and again, both arms should hang toward the golf ball rather than straight down to the ground. Having your arms hang in this fashion

50

will better enable you to get under the ball at impact, creating the loft necessary to produce consistent ball flight.

The final essential for a picture-perfect setup is the correct hip position. Your hips should be square to your shoulders, knees, and feet. If there is too much flex in your right knee, your hips will be open to the target line, which can also cause your shoulders to open and your spine to tilt toward the target. Furthermore, your weight distribution at address will be unbalanced, with too much weight on the toes of your right foot. This also forces your arms to hang too vertically. The answer is to align your hips squarely to your target line (**PHOTO 52**). Doing so will allow your spine to be properly tilted away from the target and assist in setting the shoulders and arms in the proper positions. It will also make your weight distribution more balanced. As you can see, all these elements of the pre-swing are interconnected.

Another important thing to remember is that your left hip should be slightly closer to the target than your left shoulder (**PHOTO 53**). This will ensure that your spine is correctly tilted away from the target. When your shoulders are tilted upward in the proper fashion, more of your upper body weight will rest on your right side. In order to counterbalance that weight, you should set your hips more to the left. This position will make it possible to return the club under the ball as discussed earlier.

When you achieve the correct setup position, a couple of things will be evident: 1) a line drawn from the club shaft will intersect your body at or just above your belt (**PHOTO 54**), and 2) that club shaft line will form an angle of around ninety degrees with your spine (**PHOTO 55**). If this angle is slightly greater, that's okay, as there are variances depending on an individual player's height. This is just a guideline to assist you in assuming the correct setup position. The video camera and the mirror are the perfect tools to use in checking and rechecking your pre-swing position. After you better understand the setup, you will be able to use the video camera to its full effect to work on your golf swing.

BALL POSITION

As a concept, ball position is one of the most misunderstood fundamentals in golf. Ever since the earliest days of golf instruction, students have been taught ball position in relation to the lower body—specifically, the feet. The reason is that when you take a picture of a golfer at address, you can easily zoom in on the feet and also show ball position. This has been misleading golfers for decades.

To properly understand ball position, you must relate it to your spine. I tell my students that for full swings, they should position the ball between their upper spine and left shoulder (**PHOTO 56**). For the driver and other long clubs, you can play the ball at or near your left

shoulder. For wedges and other short irons, you can play the ball as far back as the top of your spine. I will discuss ball position in more depth beginning on page 54.

It is vital to understand the importance of all these pre-swing elements. I cannot overemphasize the likelihood that just one misstep in any of these areas will create real problems. When you're examining your swing or swing flaws, you must first take a look at what you're doing in your pre-swing. As you improve your understanding of the golf swing, you will better realize how crucial the pre-swing condition is. The analogy I give to my students is an automobile. If you don't have air in the tires of your car—or gasoline or oil—the car will not run, no matter what you do. Golf is the same way. You must be meticulous in your setup position in order to make your golf swing run in a solid, consistent manner.

THE SWING

So now that you have the basics of the pre-swing, I want to share my fundamentals of the full swing. Every golf instructor applies his particular beliefs and principles when teaching. While we may tailor our lessons to the skill level and experience of the player being taught, most of us have swing theories that we have developed over time through our own experience or through exposure to other instructors. Darrell Kestner and Ted Kiegiel are two instructors who have had a tremendous impact on my teaching success. Not only are these two men great teachers, but they are also two of the best people I've had the pleasure of knowing.

I worked for Darrell at Deepdale Golf Club on Long Island from 1992 through 1995. He had a profound effect on my understanding of the golf swing as well as on the art of teaching. He taught me the importance of video technology, and I could not have written this book without the knowledge I gained from him. Ted is someone I worked with at Augusta National Golf Club. He has taught some of the top junior players in the game, including Webb Simpson, who has gone on to great success at Wake Forest University and who I am certain will have a successful professional career. Both Darrell and Ted have devoted their time and energy to becoming great instructors in the game.

There is always an explanation for what occurs when you hit a golf ball. In fact, let's start with the only real truth in golf: the clubface angle and the path of the club are the only things that affect the direction of the golf ball. The clubface is the most integral factor in the flight of a ball. At impact, the clubface must be pointing toward where you intend the ball to go, because the clubface will override the club's path. Your ball flies to the right or to the left because the face was pointed in that direction at impact. This is the inarguable truth. The speed with which the club is traveling, the quality of the hit as it relates to the sweet spot, and the path of the club will all affect the distance the ball travels, but the clubface ultimately gives the ball direction. This is why you see so many different types of swings on professional golf tours. They may look different, but they achieve the same goal: they propel the ball where the player wants it to go (most of the time).

So what is the point of explaining the importance of the clubface so early on? Because if you don't know why you are doing something, you will be less apt to commit to doing it. Further, a problem you don't understand is much more difficult to correct—you feel as if you are grasping at straws. So if you do not understand the "why" of golf, you will stray and become more confused than you were when you started. Confusion leads us to the land of poor performance. Understanding leads us out.

My fundamental belief is that in order to play consistently good golf, you must control the clubface throughout the swing. It is the most important part of the golf swing, and all analysis of your swing should be done in an effort to establish control over both the clubface and the club path. The moment the clubface reaches a poor position in the swing, you will have to compensate or alter your technique to make the ball go toward your target. I implore you to get control over the clubface first, then work on changing the club path. It is a rare situation when I will go about trying to improve a student's swing by changing the path first; I will almost always make it a priority to have a correct clubface.

Once you've corrected the clubface, you can work on correcting the club path. That will entail using the video camera to examine the path on which your club is traveling and to understand how that path is affecting the flight of the ball. Speaking of ball flight, it is important for you to understand that you can be successful with either a fade (left to right) or a draw (right to left). Working the ball both ways is nice, but if you have one reliable ball flight, you can play golf at a high level. When you're working on your swing, you must make an effort to create a consistent ball flight, whether it's a fade or a draw.

If you don't have a consistent ball flight pattern and are, in essence, starting from scratch, I would suggest that you teach yourself how to hit a draw. There are a number of reasons for this, the main one being that you will hit the ball farther. This does not mean that you cannot hit the ball far with a fade. It simply means that, as a rule, the ball will go farther with a draw because the sidespin that creates a draw often causes the ball to roll farther after landing. I want to emphasize that a large number of PGA Tour stars play with a fade, and that may in fact be the better choice for a more accomplished player. However, if you are a beginning golfer or someone struggling with the game, learn to hit a draw and you will improve.

PRACTICE

One of the biggest challenges facing all of us who play this great game is bringing our best golf game to the golf course. I've spent considerable time with a number of well-respected sports psychologists, and they have taught me a lot about how to play like you practice. I believe that most golfers are practicing the wrong way. The typical golfer goes to the practice tee and hits golf balls the way they want, but then somehow they can't perform when they go to the golf course. There is a reason for this lack of success: they may have been taught how to play, but they were never taught the correct way to practice. I'm going to share some ideas that I know will help you.

First, start with setting goals. I believe this is a critical point, and you may have been told this or even thought it yourself. It is vital to achieving success. You have to establish both short-term and long-term goals. It is okay to push yourself, but don't set unrealistic or unattainable goals. They must be challenging but also achievable.

In order to perform on the golf course, you must practice as if you were on the course. By this I mean you should imagine you are playing your home course. Play all eighteen holes. Imagine what the first hole looks like and play the hole. If it is a par four, and you would normally use your driver on the tee shot, then tee the ball up and hit the driver. Follow this procedure all the way through to the eighteenth. There are many reasons for this approach, but the primary one is that you want to create some positive thoughts to reflect upon when you are actually out playing. Ben Hogan used to do this before he played in a golf tournament. I think if it's good enough for Mr. Hogan, it's probably good enough for you.

The final thing I want to discuss is practice games, which will help you improve. One great game is to imagine a fairway on the practice tee. Put ten balls aside and see how many you can hit in the fairway. Establish a goal of four out of ten. Once you're able to do that with ease, change your goal to five out of ten, and so on. This will make you feel some pressure to perform. When you're hitting eight or nine out of ten, you'll find your scores going down. You'll also become comfortable dealing with pressure or nervousness. This is only one practice game. You can create others.

Let me warn you of something: you are going to get nervous on the golf course. Whether you are on the first tee with a number of people watching you or coming down the closing holes with a chance to shoot your career low score, you are going to get nervous. If you are not comfortable being nervous, you will never reach any of your goals. Any time you can practice while nervous, you will bring a golf course environment to the practice tee, and that is the secret to performing well on the golf course. As you do these games more often and perform them more successfully, your game will improve and your scores will be lower.

CHAPTER SUMMARY

- Your grip, posture, and ball position must all be fundamentally sound in order for you to make the swing you want. You must be diligent in checking these pre-swing keys.
- The clubface is the most important factor influencing the flight and direction of the golf ball.
- Set practice goals and stick to them. Spend some of your practice time using games to simulate golf course situations.

CHAPTER THREE

Checking Your Pre-Swing

N ow that you know how to set up the camera and you have some understanding of pre-swing and in-swing fundamentals, it's time to begin the analysis. Start with a full breakdown of your pre-swing position before you move on to actually swinging the club and hitting a golf ball. Though your pre-swing is essentially static, the video camera is very useful for noticing changes in it from day to day or week to week. Recording your pre-swing will also allow you to draw lines on the screen that will ensure you are setting up in the proper manner.

POSTURE: FACE-ON (PHOTO 57)

When I ask my students to set up to the ball, I look for a number of things relating to their posture. As in both pre-swing and in-swing analysis, I always start from the ground and work my way up. This will be the easiest way for you to remember what you have to work on, and I suggest you adopt this approach.

First, let's talk about the width of your stance. This will change with each club—it will be narrower with the shorter clubs and wider with

the longer clubs. However, on any full-swing shot, your stance should never be narrower than your hips. The outsides of your hips should always be inside your feet. In order to transfer your weight, no matter what sport you are playing, your feet must be outside of your hips. As I described earlier, the only time your feet are underneath your hips is when you are moving your weight up and down, such as when shooting a jump shot in basketball. Golf is a game of weight transfer along the ground, not up and down. Any up-and-down movement in your swing can hinder you from maximizing clubhead speed, making repeatedly good contact, and creating a consistently balanced swing.

The next element you should examine is your knees. Your left knee will appear to be taller than your right knee. This is because your hips are positioned off-center and angled toward your left foot. If you were to draw lines from the outsides of your hips down to the ground, you would notice that your left hip lines up near the instep of your left foot, while your right hip is about two inches inside your right heel (**PHOTO 58**). Also, your left shoulder should be about three inches higher than your right shoulder (**PHOTO 59**). Likewise, your spine will have a slight tilt away from the target, toward your right side. Called the "reverse K," this is the preferred setup position because in golf, your right hand is naturally set lower than your left hand. The position of your hands corresponds directly to the position of your shoulders, meaning your right shoulder will be lower than your left shoulder. Your spine will tilt away from the target, and your shoulder line will angle upward.

This upper body posture distributes more upper body weight to your right side, so your lower body must counterbalance that weight. If I were to assign a percentage of weight distribution at address, I would say that for your lower body it should be 60 percent on your left side and

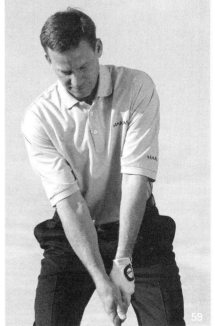

40 percent on your right side, whereas for your upper body it should be 60 percent on your right side and 40 percent on your left. Of course, this is not an exact science, but as long as you get the point that your lower body will have more weight on your left side and your upper body will have more weight on your right side, you'll be in good shape. Again, this basic concept is due to the mechanics of the golf grip, in which your right hand is lower. Therefore, your shoulders, hips, knees, and feet must be aligned in a corresponding way.

The final consideration in this face-on view is the angle of the club shaft. I believe that the shaft should point in between your neck and your left shoulder (**PHOTO 60**). This position will place the club's handle closer to the target than the clubhead, giving the shaft a forward lean. That is exactly the condition you want to have at impact, which is why

it is so important to set the shaft that way at address. While the degree of forward lean will vary with each club, remember that the club should never, ever lean backward when making contact with the ball. When you're hitting a driver, because of the ball position it may appear that the shaft is leaning backward, as shown in photo 60. At address the shaft of the driver may lean backward a small amount, but at impact it should lean forward one to two degrees. You will notice from the picture that the shaft of the golf club is pointing toward the left armpit, aligned with the ball position.

POSTURE: DOWN THE LINE (**PHOTO 61**)

From the down-the-line view, you should first take a look at your knee flex. You want to see your knees bent slightly, so that they are over the saddles of your shoes and your rear end is four to six inches past your heels. Your back should be basically flat and straight, but because your arms are reaching in front of your body, your back may appear to curve into what I call the "butterfly," which is nothing more than the back spreading out from side to side. It is important to be able to notice the difference between a rounded back (which you should avoid) and a butterfly back. When your back gets rounded, it spreads out from top to bottom, and your belt line will appear to be nearly parallel to the ground (**PHOTO 62**). When your back is in the correct position, your belt line will angle toward the ground (**PHOTO 63**). Your arms, meanwhile, should extend out slightly so that if you drew a line from your chin to the ground, it would go through your right hand and continue to the ball side of the toe line (**PHOTO 64**). The amount your arms extend will vary as the clubs get longer or shorter. However, you do not want to set your arms too vertical or too horizontal, and drawing this line will assist you with finding the proper arm extension.

The next consideration is the shaft plane line, a line that runs up the shaft of the club through your body. The shaft plane line should intersect with your belt line or just slightly above it, as I discussed earlier. Finally, take a good look at your head position. Your head should appear to be a normal extension of your spine, which doesn't happen when your chin is buried into your chest (**PHOTO 65**). Make sure there is enough room between your chin and chest so that you can make a fist and fit your hand in there comfortably (**PHOTO 66**).

Once you have checked your body positions as they relate to posture, take a look at the alignment of your feet, knees, hips, and shoulders. All four of these elements must be parallel to one another. The most important are your hips and shoulders. I am adamant about this—make sure that your shoulder line and your hip line are parallel not only to each other but also to your target line. You may have heard that it is okay if your shoulder line is open to your hip line, but I feel this is the biggest posture error you can make, and the most

common mistake among high-handicap players. The majority of these players slice the ball, and in my opinion, this is largely because their shoulder lines are open at address. It is essential to understand that if your shoulders are open, you are going to have an outside-to-inside swing path, which will likely create a slice. So to avoid this damaging swing flaw, align your shoulders parallel to your hips. From the down-the-line camera angle, you will know you are setting up correctly if the top part of your left arm is above your right arm (**PHOTO 67**). Also, you should be able to see the top part of your left thigh above your right thigh (**PHOTO 68**). If you cannot see your left thigh, you have too much weight on your right leg at address, and therefore too much upper-body weight on your right leg. As a result, your hips and shoulders will be open to the intended target.

BALL POSITION: FACE-ON (**PHOTO 69**)

Ball position is one of the hardest concepts to understand and, in my view, the most poorly taught fundamental in the game. You have probably heard ball position taught using the lower body as a reference. In that context, you position the ball either closer to or farther from your left foot, or perhaps even near the "center of your stance." The problem with this method is that your feet have nothing to do with ball position. The ball's true position is in relation to your spine, and specifically your upper spine. Depending on the club you're using, your ball position should be set somewhere between your spine and your left armpit. **PHOTO 70** shows how I want you to think of ball position—always relative to the upper body. When hitting longer clubs, you should position the ball closer to your armpit, or more "forward." With shorter clubs, you should position the ball more toward your spine, or more "back."

Here comes the hard part. When your shoulder line changes (becomes more open or closed to the target line), the ball position changes as well. So if your shoulder line opens, which is the most common mistake when hitting a driver, the ball position actually moves back. Remember from the last paragraph that you want the ball position *forward* when using longer clubs, so you can see where this would cause a problem. Conversely, when your shoulder line gets closed, the ball position shifts forward. Again, this is not a good thing. The way to see this relationship between your shoulder line and ball position is to imagine a perpendicular line extending from your shoulder line at the top of your spine. I have used a golf club in the following pictures to illustrate this. In **PHOTO 71**, you can see the golf ball directly in line with the club shaft, with the shaft perpendicular to the shoulder line. This is what I will call a middle ball position because it is directly in line with my spine. Now, in **PHOTO 72**, I have maintained the same position with my feet but rotated my shoulders into an open position. It is clear that the golf ball has moved back relative to my spine, because the club shaft is now to the left of the golf ball. In **PHOTO 73**, the club shaft is now to

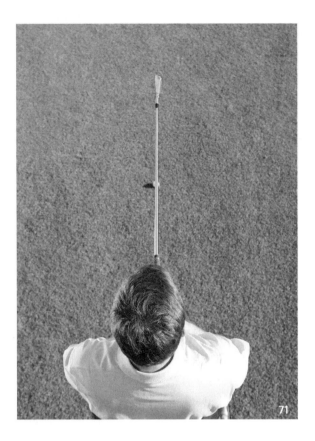

the right of the golf ball, which puts the ball forward. You can see that when the alignment of the shoulders changes, the ball position moves either forward or backward, depending on that alignment, despite the ball not changing location on the ground.

It is important to understand that ball position and shoulder alignment are related, and you cannot look at one without looking at the other. I believe that problems occur mostly with the longer clubs—drivers, fairway woods, hybrids, and long irons—because many people have been instructed to move the ball forward in their stance or toward their left foot with these clubs. When you do that and then reach for the ball, your shoulder line opens up and the flaws multiply. You suddenly become out of position because you have effectively moved the ball back, which causes a variety of ball flight patterns, most of which go anywhere other than the desired direction. Since most of the shots you're hitting require those longer clubs, you play terribly, complain to your spouse or local PGA professional, and eventually buy a bowling ball! I want to stop this insanity now and impress upon you how important ball position is and how it can affect everything from your setup to your full swing, and ultimately, your attitude. Make sure to examine your ball position every time you practice and ensure that it is in the right place relative to your upper body, not to your lower body.

So what is the correct ball position? The simple answer is, it depends on the club you're hitting. As a general rule, for all of your wedges and up through your 7-iron, the correct ball position will be just forward of your spine. For your 6-iron through 4-iron, the ball should be positioned two inches forward of your spine. For fairway woods and hybrids, the ball should be three inches forward of your spine, and for

the driver, it should be positioned below your left armpit. These are standard ball positions, and they should not be altered until you are able to break 75 on a consistent basis. When you reach that point with your game, you may move the ball position around in order to change either the trajectory or the ball flight. I would suggest that you focus on building good, solid fundamentals—which includes using the standard ball positions—and not do too much experimentation until your game has reached a higher level.

CHAPTER SUMMARY

- In order to properly transfer your weight, you must place your feet wider than your hips at address.
- Once you check your posture, ensure that your feet, knees, hips, and shoulders are parallel to one another.
- Think of ball position as it relates to your upper body rather than to your stance.

CHAPTER FOUR

Analyzing Your Golf Swing

Learning how to analyze your golf swing using the video camera will take some time. Once you know what you're looking for, however, you will be able to pinpoint your faults and figure out how to correct them. You will also be able to chart your progress.

As I explain the various positions that make up the golf swing, understand that your technique can be rated in an allowable plus-minus range. In other words, there is perfect form, and there is acceptable form. The better a player you become, the more you will understand the difference and the lower your tolerance for mistakes will be. However, you must understand what you are looking for and how the motion of the golf club affects the flight of the golf ball.

Finally—and I will continue to emphasize this point throughout the book—the pre-swing is as important as the actual swing. I don't dispute that it is essential to examine your golf swing on video and attempt to correct its flaws, but I would like to make the point that if you fail to position yourself properly prior to hitting the golf ball, there is a better-than-average chance the ball will not go where you want it to. Further, a poor setup will lead to inconsistency in both contact and shot results. Once you have learned those concepts, your swing will improve steadily.

SWING POSITION 1: ADDRESS

FACE-ON (**PHOTO 74**)

Here is a friendly reminder: Your setup, or posture, affects everything in your golf swing, so how you address the ball should be the first step of your analysis. If you are unfamiliar with the concepts of a proper setup or do not completely understand them, go back and reread the previous chapter. When I'm giving a lesson, I always look first at the student's address position, whether the person is a beginner or a scratch player. Further, no matter how many times I've taught a particular student, I examine their setup to start the lesson, because they may have unintentionally altered some aspect of their setup since our last lesson. You may have worked on your setup last week but then had to wait a week to set up your camera and begin the swing analysis. If that is the case, you need to start your session with a setup review. I look closely at grip, body position, alignment, ball position, and weight distribution—and you should, too. These elements are critical to the success of your golf swing, so you must ensure that your setup position is correct. Never underestimate the importance of setup.

SWING POSITION 2: CLUB PARALLEL TO GROUND

FACE-ON (**PHOTO 75**)

About halfway into your backswing, the club should be nearly parallel to the ground. As you pause the video camera here and look at your position from the face-on angle, there are a couple of points of interest. The primary one is the relationship between your left arm and your wrist. Let me first address the arm: there is an angle created at

address between the club shaft and your left forearm. Depending on the length of the club and your hand size, arm length, height, and some other factors, this angle will vary. When the club moves away from the golf ball, a small amount of wrist hinge will occur, creating an angle of around 135 degrees when the club shaft is nearly parallel to the ground (**PHOTO 76**). I look for the end of the club's handle to be above your back foot. Again, the location of the club handle will vary slightly depending upon the individual and the club being used. If you are hitting a driver and the end of the handle is inside your back foot instead of over it, that is acceptable. Understand that this is an attempt to give you guidance; you do not have to be perfect. The greater the angle between your forearm and the club shaft at address, the farther past the back foot the handle's end will be in this position. Regardless, you should make it a goal to get the club hinged and create an angle of around 135 degrees.

At this point and from this angle, you should be able to see some space between your forearms. If you cannot, then your wrists have not hinged, or set, properly. This occurs for a number of reasons. First, it could be an issue of strength. I've found that people who lack hand strength have a difficult time hinging the club properly. It is not always the case, but it is a concern. Second, your grip could be faulty. A simple way to determine this is to look at the thumb and index finger on your left hand. If you have what I call a "short thumb," where the knuckle of your index finger is on the same line as the tip of your thumb (**PHOTO 77**), your ability to hinge the club will be greatly inhibited.

However, the most common cause of poor wrist set is too much shoulder turn or hip turn early in the swing. For quite a few years now, you've read and heard that the more you turn the body, the more power you'll create. While this is true in some cases, turning can more often cause

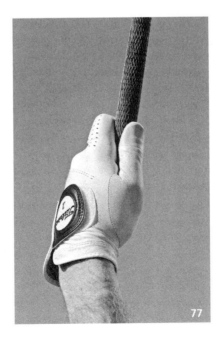

you to move the club in what I call an "around-and-up" motion—when you fail to hinge your wrists at the correct time in the backswing and the clubhead remains too close to the ground (**PHOTO 78**). As a result, when it is time to move the club above your waist, it is too far behind you. This fault is more obvious in the down-the-line view, which I will look at next. I will say, though, that this problem was prevalent among my students when I first took the head professional job at Sunningdale Country Club. If you see this fault in your swing on video, don't despair. It is common and can be solved. Just remember: the golf swing combines around and up movements *at the same time*. The swing will not function properly or produce consistently good shots if one occurs before the other. You must have both motions at the same time.

SWING POSITION 2: CLUB PARALLEL TO GROUND

DOWN THE LINE (**PHOTO 79**)

There are a number of elements to consider when you examine the second swing position from the camera's down-the-line view. First, you are looking for a "short shaft"—this means that there should be a small amount of, if any, club shaft visible. If you were to draw on the video screen a circle that includes your hands, the club shaft, and the club-head, that circle would be very small (**PHOTO 80**). The smaller the circle, the better your position at this point in the swing.

Further, you want to see that the club shaft is parallel to your toe line and on or to the ball side of it. Also, your left arm and the club shaft should be lined up with each other when seen from this view. I'm not overly concerned with the position of the clubface unless it is dramatically closed (facing down to the ground) or dramatically open (facing up to the sky). I prefer the toe of the club to be over the heel of the club, as in photo 80. However, once again, as long as the clubface is close to this position, it's okay. Clubface position varies from player to player due to differences in how they hinge the club back. The most important position for the clubface in the backswing is at the top of the swing, which I will examine in detail later in this chapter. What is important here is that the clubface has not done anything dramatically poor to this point.

At this point, your hips and shoulders will have turned a little bit. The chest and shoulders will have rotated more than the hips, which is desirable. Your knee flex will also be similar to what it was at address; however, your knees will have rotated just a little back toward the camera. Again, there is not much rotation, but it is somewhat noticeable.

Finally, you should be able to clearly see both of your arms in front of your body. This is critical, for if your arms have moved behind your hip line as in **PHOTO 81**, you will not have enough space to drop your arms and the club into the correct downswing position known as "the slot." In order to get your arms into the correct position in front of your body, some forearm rotation must occur in this initial part of the backswing. Remember, you are going to move the club both up and around, and if you have no forearm rotation, the club will likely do one or the other but not both.

SWING POSITION 3: LEFT ARM PARALLEL TO GROUND

FACE-ON (PHOTO 82)

You have now begun to hinge the club, and the angle created by your left arm and the club shaft is around ninety degrees. Many successful touring professionals have less than ninety degrees, while others have more. Nevertheless, as a rule, you are looking for around ninety degrees. Even if you have a little more or a little less, the key here is to make sure that the club is moving into a hinged position.

There are some other concepts to take note of at this point in the swing. Your shoulders should have rotated at least sixty-five degrees but should not have reached their maximum turn. If you have a ninety-degree shoulder turn at the top of your swing and at this point your shoulders have turned seventy-five degrees, that's fine. The point is that you should have most of your shoulder turn, but not all of it. The reason is that your arms and shoulders should stop turning at the same time—i.e., at the top of the backswing. If you max out your shoulder turn before that, your swing will be out of sync.

Another important aspect at this point in the swing is your head, which should have maintained the same level it had at address. This can be measured by drawing a horizontal line under your chin at address. It is okay for your head to move laterally during the swing, but it should not move down below this line as you swing the club back (**PHOTO 83**). Dipping your head toward the ball will move weight toward your toes during the backswing. When that happens, your swing is in major trouble, because you will lift your weight upward through impact, forcing the club to reroute itself dramatically on its path to the ball, either under the preferred swing plane or over it. Also, your

weight will not move toward the target like it should, resulting in a variety of mis-hit shots.

Two more elements you want to pay attention to are your hips and your knees. Their positions are related, which is why I mention them together. First, your right hip should rotate—not slide. You can monitor this by drawing vertical lines from your belt line down to the ground at both outer edges of your hips at address. You should notice that your right hip will have turned but will not have moved outside the line (**PHOTO 84**). Likewise, your right knee will move, but again, not outside the line. The amount of space between the knees will be almost the same as there was at address, with your left knee outside of your left hip. Your left hip will move slightly away from the vertical line you drew, but I emphasize *slightly*. A large amount of space between the line and your left hip at this point indicates an over-rotation of your hips, and likely of your shoulders as well. The cure for this is to hit balls with your knees bowed out (a drill you will find in chapter five) so there is weight on the outsides of both of your feet (**PHOTO 85**). I call this the John Wayne drill. Hit balls from this position, and you will significantly reduce the over-rotation of your lower body.

The last point of emphasis in this frame is the weight shift. Specifically, you want to learn how to avoid a reverse pivot. At this point in the swing, you will begin to see what a reverse pivot looks like if you have one. Your hips will move toward the target and your head will be to the target side of the ball. The majority of your weight will appear to be on your left side (**PHOTO 86**). Furthermore, your left knee will move forward (toward your toes) and your head will look as if it's dropping. It is! This is the classic reverse pivot—a death move in the golf swing, because in order to create power, you must load your weight onto your right leg in the backswing. When you swing with a reverse pivot, you have moved your weight in a reverse fashion, causing more problems than you care to know about. Suffice it to say, there is no sport where the weight moves toward the target in the windup and away from the

target in the delivery. Think of walking. If you were to walk forward and lean backward, how effective would that be? Not very effective at all. The golf swing is the same. Simply put, your weight should move in the same direction the club moves. Understand this, and you are well on your way to a sound golf swing.

SWING POSITION 3: LEFT ARM PARALLEL TO GROUND

DOWN THE LINE (PHOTO 87)

The down-the-line view of the third swing position is very important for a variety of reasons. Most noticeably, it is the first time we see the club in an upside-down position, and so the relationship of the club to

the shaft plane becomes extremely important. Since we're analyzing the full swing, we must be aware of the shaft plane. I will explain the shaft plane in more detail a little later on.

Let's work again from the ground up and point out what you should take note of in this view. You should have maintained your knee flex and not over-turned your hips. These should be a constant at this point in the swing. As long as those are correct, we can move on to the fun parts.

We'll begin with your spine angle. Go back to the view of your address position and draw a line from your ear down to your hip (**PHOTO 88**). This is your spine angle, and it is very important to maintain a consistent spine angle throughout the swing. The angle will change depending on the length of the club you're swinging, but it is usually around forty degrees. Whatever your measurement is at the start of your swing, you want to feel as if you are maintaining that spine angle from address through impact.

When analyzing this position further, you will notice a couple of things. First, in a correct swing, you will have maintained your spine angle, meaning that the line you drew from your ear at address still passes through your ear at this point in the swing (**PHOTO 89**). Your forearms should be parallel to the ground, and the butt end of your club should point at or near the target line. I like the shaft to point above the target line as pictured, but just slightly. As the left forearm rotates in the backswing, the shaft of the golf club will be parallel to the shaft plane.

Additionally, take note of your hand position at this point in the swing. The triangle formed by your left shoulder, right elbow and right

shoulder is extremely important. Every great player from Nicklaus to Woods will have one or both hands in this triangle (**PHOTO 90**). Establishing the correct position with your hands here will allow your wrists to hinge correctly and will help bring the club shaft to the top of the swing on the proper plane. It is another way to ensure your hands and arms are in front of your chest. And, because of your wrist hinge, the most important element, the clubface, will most certainly be square when the club arrives at the top of the backswing. Further, your right elbow will fold properly, creating the space necessary for the hands and arms to fall into the downswing.

This frame also shows the width in the backswing arc. Width is the amount of distance between your chest and your hands. If your hands are not in front of your chest, the width decreases. The triangle I discussed in the last paragraph is critical in describing width. If your hands stray either below or above the triangle, your swing width decreases and you lose power. I'm a big believer in width for a couple of reasons: First, it assists with creating proper tempo. When your chest and arms move together, it slows the backswing and allows for proper tempo. Second, it allows for maximum clubhead speed on the downswing. When I begin to discuss the downswing, I will talk about "downloading," which refers to the storing, or in some cases creating, of additional clubhead speed. This will have a direct effect on your potential distance. I say "potential" because actual distance is a combination of many different factors, and clubhead speed is only one of them. Regardless, the width you create on your backswing is important, and keeping your hands within this triangle is an indication that you've established the right amount of width. Of all the players I've studied, Tiger Woods is the best at this. Work on establishing the width in your swing, and you will be on your way to creating some distance in your game. The reason that golf has become a game of distance and power is the increased focus on swing width, in contrast to the narrower swings prevalent a few decades ago.

SWING POSITION 4: TOP OF THE BACKSWING

FACE-ON (**PHOTO 91**)

As you examine your top-of-the-swing position, focus first on your feet and knees rather than on the club. In the modern golf swing, both feet remain on the ground in order to limit the over-rotation of the hips. This was not the case with swings of forty to fifty years ago—Jack Nicklaus, for example, was taught to allow his left heel to come off the ground. While this worked for Jack, it is not considered ideal today. Unless you have limited flexibility, you should keep your left foot completely on the ground. If flexibility is a problem, allow your left heel to come off the ground just slightly as you swing to the top. However, doing so can create some swing flaws on the downswing, so I would recommend this only as a last resort.

A number of good players have had success with rotating their left knee back underneath their left hip at the top of the backswing (**PHOTO 92**). However, your knee should rotate back as little as possible, so that it remains outside your left hip, as in photo 91. The concept is similar to that of keeping your left heel on the ground: The less your knees move, the greater the stability of your lower body. What you want is a very quiet lower body without much movement in your feet and knees.

Once you've achieved this quiet lower body, you should make a couple of observations when you freeze the frame of yourself at the top of the swing. First, your right leg should be angled slightly toward the target. Also, your right hip should be inside your right foot and your

hips should have turned no more than forty-five degrees. Remember, you want hip turn but not over-rotation.

Now shift your focus to your upper body at the top of the back-swing. Here's where the real fun begins, because this is a major part of the overall swing and significantly determines the actual result of the shot. First, notice the angle of your back as you hold the club at the top. You should see an angle that is about fifteen degrees and leaning away from the target, meaning that your back is facing more to the sky than to the ground (**PHOTO 93**). This angle is essential in loading your weight properly onto your back foot. You will also notice that your head has moved back a bit from where it was at ad-dress. The position of the head will depend on the club you're using and the width of your stance. However, the loading of weight onto your right leg is no different. There must be a move to the right leg regardless of the club.

You should strive to have your left arm at an angle of around sixty-five degrees with the driver and then decrease it as the clubs get shorter. Further, you should see some space between your head and hands; this is a position you should work hard to achieve. Some instructors refer to the position of the left arm in relation to the hand of a clock. This sixty-five-degree angle would be around eleven o'clock if twelve o'clock is perpendicular to the ground. There is a belief that the farther your left arm travels, the farther the ball will travel, which is true to a point. Some players can generate more power when their arm travels past the eleven o'clock position. However, swinging your arm farther back is not always conducive to producing clubhead speed. In fact, many players will lose leverage in their downswing if they swing back too far, and the clubhead will actually slow down while approaching the golf ball. I will discuss leverage and clubhead speed in more detail in the section about the downswing.

One final question you might be asking: How much angle should there be between your left arm and the club shaft at the top of the swing? Good question! The angle should be around ninety degrees. Again, there are players who can generate more clubhead speed with less than ninety degrees and others who can benefit from going to a greater angle. However, ninety degrees should be your goal.

SWING POSITION 4: TOP OF THE BACKSWING

DOWN THE LINE (**PHOTO 94**)

This is a classic position. Think of the most memorable golf photographs; many were taken at the top of the backswing from the down-the-line angle. So much can be seen from this view, which is why this is one of my favorite positions to discuss. It is an extremely informative snapshot, as a proper backswing prepares you for the downswing. Again, start from the ground up.

Your right knee should have maintained its flex. When you do this correctly, you won't be able to see any daylight between your kneecaps (**PHOTO 95**). As you saw from the face-on angle, your hips should have

turned approximately forty-five degrees, or as far as you can comfortably rotate them. If at address you drew a line at a ninety-degree angle
to the ground that touched your rear end, in this position your butt
should have stayed in contact with or just inside that line (**PHOTOS 96
AND 97**). If it did, your weight distribution is balanced between your
heels and toes.

More vital information can be gleaned by drawing two other lines
on the screen. First, draw a shaft plane line from address that extends
from the hosel of the golf club, up the club shaft, and straight back
to the level of your head (**PHOTO 98**). At the top of your backswing,
the elbow of your right arm should be on or slightly above the shaft
plane line (**PHOTO 99**). Next, draw a line along your left forearm at
the top of the swing. This line should be nearly parallel to the shaft
plane line. Further, your left arm should rest on or above your right

shoulder. Some players have had great success letting their left arm rise above their right shoulder, including the likes of Jack Nicklaus and Fred Couples. So if you notice your arm is in a similar position, that is fine and no cause for concern, as long as your arm is not blocking your ear (**PHOTO 100**). If it is, your arm is beyond what I would call the maximum allowable steepness. When your hands get that high in the backswing, the angle of attack in your downswing will also be too steep, causing a variety of mis-hit shots that I am certain you will not enjoy. The only way to make this arm position work will be to reroute the club in a looping fashion on the downswing in order to get it back on plane. Unless your name is Jim Furyk, that is a very tall order. My suggestion is that it is easier to correct this flaw in your backswing than to try and compensate for it in the downswing.

100

The other cause for concern is an arm position that's too shallow, which happens when your left arm is below your shoulder line at the top (**PHOTO 101**). Again, I could recite all the bad things that can occur when you get into this position, but I would rather save you some reading time and suggest that you fix it by getting your left arm higher. Just remember that the position of your left arm at the top of your backswing has a sizable and recognizable effect on the position of the clubface and the path of your downswing—that is the most important concept I can convey to you about this position.

The next elements to discuss are the clubface position and the shaft position at the top of the backswing. Regarding the clubface, keep in mind that you want to achieve a "square" face at the top. Terminology in golf instruction is critically important, and the word "square" is used

routinely among golfers and teachers. So it's worth a minute to clearly define the use of "square" as it applies to the clubface at the top of the backswing. When I say "square," I'm talking about the relationship of the clubface angle to your left arm. For instance, if your left arm at the top has an angle of forty-five degrees, then a square clubface would also have an angle of forty-five degrees (**PHOTO 102**). This is easily monitored by drawing a line along your left arm and then drawing another along the clubface. You want these lines to be parallel to each other and nearly parallel to the shaft plane line as shown in photo 98 (on page 83). You'll notice that the clubface is square when your left wrist is flat. Cupping (**PHOTO 103**) or bowing (**PHOTO 104**) your left wrist will directly affect the angle of the clubface. Therefore, the way to fix a clubface that is not square is to work on your left wrist position at the top of your swing. I would advise you not to think about it unless you notice that you have the clubface in a poor position when you pause the video of your swing. There are some talented players whose grip is less than

ideal but who manage to square the clubface at the top by manipulating their wrist on the way back. This has been done successfully by the likes of Fred Couples and Paul Azinger, both of whom have won major championships. This approach promotes inconsistency in the average player, however, and I wouldn't suggest using it.

Finally, you should examine the position of the club shaft at the top of your swing. The shaft position will vary with each club—the longer the club, the longer the swing. Unless you're hitting a driver, the clubhead should always be farther from the ball than the grip. When you execute this properly, a line drawn down the shaft will always point toward or inside the ball line. With a driver, the proper position from this angle will make it look as if there is no shaft at all because the shaft will be pointing directly toward the camera. This will occur because the shaft is parallel to the ground and on plane, so it will be parallel to the target line as well. If the driver shaft is short of parallel, that is also fine—in fact, for many amateurs, it is preferred, because they often overswing and get out of sync. As long as your shoulders have turned completely and the rest of the positions discussed thus far are good, swinging the driver short of parallel will work. Again, it's important to remember that there are ideal guidelines for a proper swing, but as long as your positions are close, you will be all right.

SWING POSITION 5: THE TRANSITION

FACE-ON (**PHOTO 105**)

If impact is the moment of truth, then this next sequence of frames involves the motion that helps you find it. Your position as the club changes direction and begins the downswing is very important, because it leads directly to impact. All great players have this in common: their body begins to move into the downswing while the club is still moving in the backswing. When you look at yourself on video during this portion of the swing, the space between your knees should be wider than it was at address (**PHOTO 106**) and certainly wider than at the top of the swing (**PHOTO 107**). This widening is due to the forward movement of your left knee and the decreasing of the angle between your thighs and chest, the latter of which is better seen in the down-the-line view and will be discussed later in the chapter. There should

also be forward movement in your hips during the transition, while at the same time your hips should start to unwind as well. At this point, both of your feet should be firmly planted on the ground (**PHOTO 108**).

You will notice the shaft of the club drop a bit and get closer to your head than it was at the top of the swing. It will also appear that the angle between your left arm and the shaft has decreased. The decrease of this angle is called "downloading," and it transfers the power you stored in the backswing to your downswing. When you download, you allow for a whipping action of the club shaft, which will maximize your clubhead's speed when it contacts the golf ball.

From this face-on view, you should also begin to see your right shoulder, while your upper body should be sinking. If you draw a line across the top of your head at the top of the swing, you will notice there is more space between your head and the line during the transition, because your upper body drops down while it squares up to the target line. The average Tour professional will drop one to two inches during the transition, and this should be a goal for you as well. The drop happens because your chest squares up to the ball while moving into what is called a "stacked" position, meaning your upper body has shifted forward into the center of your stance. You should also notice the movement of your head toward the target. If you draw a line on the right side of your head at the top of the backswing, you will notice the space here in the transition has increased.

Golf is no different from any other sport in which you are moving an object forward: when you transfer your weight correctly, your head and body move in the same direction as the ball. However, there is one major difference between the mechanics of golf and those of other ball-related sports. Simply, you don't have to help the ball into the air, because the club does the work for you. Many amateur golfers struggle with this concept—they fail to move their body in a forward direction because of their desire to hit the golf ball into the air. The common mistake is to move your body up and back, rather than down and forward. If you commit this critical error, you won't see your body moving forward toward the target during the transition. The root cause of this misplaced desire to help the ball get into the air is the fact that the golf ball is sitting on the ground. In normal circumstances, when you attempt to get anything into the air, there is an upward motion of your body. Further, if you've played sports requiring you to throw or hit a ball, that instinct has been reinforced. A natural opening of the chest to the sky occurs. *In fact, this is the exact opposite of what should happen in golf.* When you swing the club correctly, your head and chest will move forward and down, and the ball will have no problem getting airborne.

Many amateurs who make this mistake also lose power in their golf swing during the transition. When your head and body move backward, the club shaft will tend to "bounce" up at the start of the downswing. That bounce refers to the angle between your left arm and the club shaft—if it increases during transition (**PHOTO 109**), you will lose clubhead speed and therefore power. One of the common traits seen in all great players is the ability to maintain or decrease the angle between their left forearm and the club shaft during transition. This is how the club shaft loads power for impact, and it allows for maximum clubhead speed. It is what separates the professionals and accomplished amateurs from the majority of golfers.

SWING POSITION 5: THE TRANSITION

DOWN THE LINE (**PHOTO 110**)

This frame shows a number of important elements. First, as I've discussed previously, your head will have dropped from where it was at the top of the swing. When you draw a line on the screen across the top of your head as you completed the backswing (**PHOTO 111**), you notice that your head is below that line in this frame (**PHOTO 112**). You do not want your head to get closer to the ball, only closer to the ground. Leaning forward and getting your head closer to the ball will put too much weight on your toes. Your knees and hips should also have squared to the target line to allow for proper weight transition. Your spine angle should also have been maintained, which is one of the most important things to look for when you're struggling. You

can monitor this by drawing a line down your spine from your ear to your pants pocket as I described earlier.

In this down-the-line view, you should also pay close attention to the movement of your rear end. When reviewing your swing, first draw a line from your butt to the ground at the address position (**PHOTO 113**). The difference between great ball strikers and poor ones relates to the movement of the rear end from address through the remainder of the swing. In these frames you will notice the difference between proper and improper motion of the rear end. When your butt stays on the line, your spine can maintain a proper tilt. When your butt comes off the line (**PHOTO 114**), your spine angle changes and your chest begins to move away from the golf ball. In this photo, you can see that my right hip is over my right foot. This is a direct indication that I have changed my spine angle. What you should further notice is that my head has risen up because my spine angle has become nearly perpendicular to the ground with the hips moving toward the ball.

I will explain this point in further detail because it's the most important element of the transition as seen from the down-the-line view. A golf swing, like other athletic motions, requires balance in order to be effective. Because of the materials and design of the equipment used in golf, however, you are going to be able to hit a golf ball farther than you would any other object in any other sport. Consider that a baseball well hit by a home-run hitter can sometimes travel 450 feet. That is a home run in any ballpark in the world, and yet it translates to a shot of only 150 yards, which is achievable with a mid-iron for most golfers. A human being could never propel a tennis ball or hockey puck that far. The longest field goal in the history of the National Football League is sixty-three yards. The point is, you are moving the golf ball a very long way without stepping, striding, or running. You're going to take a club, turn it upside down, and strike a ball that is 1.68 inches in diameter with a clubface that is no longer

than five inches from heel to toe. You are going to attempt to control the ball so that it goes where you want it to go, and when it doesn't, you are going to wonder why. My favorite part of the whole process is when my students say, "This game should not be that hard because the ball is not moving." I know it isn't, but every part of your body, and the club, *are* moving. That is the supreme challenge of golf and why balance in the transition is so important.

In an average swing, your club is moving at around eighty miles per hour and you are trying to keep your balance. So there are two objectives in the golf swing, and both are at a critical juncture in the transition: hit the golf ball and maintain balance. The only thing you should be conscious of is the swinging of the club. After all, you developed balance at a very young age, and you shouldn't have to stop and think about it anymore. It is instinctual. In fact, your subconscious mind is always trying to maintain balance, sometimes at the expense of whatever activity you're engaged in. Imagine walking on a sidewalk curb; your goal is to stay on the curb and not fall off. When you begin to lose balance and come close to falling off the curb, your subconscious mind will take over and you will actually stop walking and steady yourself using your arms and legs. The act of walking is quickly abandoned when your balance is compromised. When your body makes an improper move during the golf swing, your brain will give up on making the correct swing in order to maintain balance, just like it gave up on walking when you were about to fall off the curb. This is not to say you can't hit a good shot with poor balance once in a while. However, doing so will be as likely as rolling double sixes. It can happen—just not often enough. When you move out of balance, your swing is compromised. To improve your golf game, you must make sure your balance is consistently good. The contrast between a free-flowing golf swing and one made when you fall out of balance will be very apparent on video.

Don't take advice on balance just from me. There is a book I strongly recommend—consider it a fun homework assignment—that addresses the importance of balance and how to achieve it. Called *Balanced Golf*, it's written by Ted Kiegiel. Ted is a martial arts expert who holds several black belts. Discussing the importance of the "tower of balance," he describes "the inability to create effective motion if one's tower of balance crumbles." In other words, negatively affected balance makes a negative impact on your swing. I've known Ted for close to twenty years now, and there are few, if any, other golf professionals who possess his level of understanding of both martial arts and the golf swing. The mere fact that there is a book titled *Balanced Golf* suggests the importance of this element to your swing.

I hope you now understand how important balance is to the entire golf swing and how the transition is the crucial moment when your balance can either be sustained or go awry. Further, the transition provides a key snapshot of your spine angle and shows why maintaining it is vital to a consistent golf swing. These factors directly affect the path of your club and its condition at impact.

SWING POSITION 6: HALFWAY DOWN

FACE-ON (PHOTO 115)

In this view, your hands should be just outside your right thigh and over the right foot. This is a classic position—very dynamic, exciting, and full of movement. Showing how your hands lead the clubhead into the ball, it reveals the true source of power in the golf swing: the fact that the clubhead lags behind and then reaches maximum speed at impact. This position is also a key to determining the initial direction of the shot, because at this point in the swing, the clubface is rotating quickly from open to (hopefully) square at impact, which will send the ball toward your intended target. There are a number of key points to examine when looking at this position from the face-on view, most prominently the angle between your left forearm and the club shaft. However, let's first look at what's happening throughout your body.

Even though this position is just a few frames past the transition, quite a bit has happened. Your knees should have rotated toward the target and your right foot should be starting to lift off the ground. Because of these movements, your weight should have shifted to the insides of your feet, and your right heel may even be slightly off the ground. Your hips should have also rotated to the point where your belt buckle faces the target side of the ball. Your chest should be facing slightly behind the ball, and your head should be positioned between the ball and your right foot.

Now let's turn our attention back to power and why this frame is so important in assessing how much power your swing can generate. Compare the positions of the left forearm and the club shaft in **PHOTOS 115 AND 116**. The obvious difference is the angles between the forearm and the club shaft. The correct angle is around 90 degrees, and the incorrect angle is around 135 degrees. The narrower the angle, the greater the potential distance. You will also notice that the underside of the right forearm is more visible with the poor technique. There also happens to be more space between the forearms, which is an indication that power is being released well before impact. This is an example of a hit rather than a swing. Despite the forceful tone of the word, the hit is not a good thing in golf, because it steals power from your swing. As a result of the hit impulse, the player's right arm is straightening out, and the "power angle," or download, between the left forearm and the club shaft is diminished. That translates to lower clubhead speed and less power.

What you will also notice in this face-on view is that the clubhead will be much higher and closer to your sternum when you are in the correct position. You can see that with the proper swing the club shaft will point just ahead of the golf ball (as in photo 115) and in an incorrect swing it will point toward the target (as in photo 116). When the power angle is retained, the clubhead will remain closer to your sternum. As the angle between your left forearm and the club shaft decreases, your amount of leverage increases. Leverage is something that provides greater strength than you might otherwise have. *Webster's Dictionary* defines leverage as the mechanical advantage gained by the action of a lever. The word "advantage" is important because if you can gain an advantage by using something, you would be smart to use it. Let's face it, we should all use every advantage possible in golf, and leverage is a huge one. It helps you create more clubhead speed and more potential distance.

116

SWING POSITION 6: HALFWAY DOWN

DOWN THE LINE (**PHOTO 117**)

In this view, your weight should move to your forward leg and your hips should rotate and square to the target line. Your head should have dropped from its address position, and your rear end should still be on the same line it was on at address, as I discussed in the analysis of the face-on view. But the primary thing I want you to focus on in this view is the relationship of the club shaft to your right forearm.

Take a look at the following pictures of swing position 6. The swing shown in **PHOTO 118** will cause the shot to hook or push away from the target; the swing in **PHOTO 119** will cause it to slice or pull away from the target. These pictures show the relationship between the club shaft

and your right forearm for these two different clubhead paths—when the shaft is too far below the right arm, the result is a severe inside-to-out path that produces either a hook or push; when it's too far above the right arm, the result is a severe outside-to-in path that produces a slice or pull. The ideal path is inside-square-inside, which happens when the club shaft is aligned with your right forearm, as in photo 117. This is the best position because it will allow you not only to hit the ball consistently well but also to easily draw and fade the ball toward your target. Again, I am talking about a slight curvature of the shot, rather than the severely off-line shots seen with the other paths. Further, the proper path will cause the ball to start its flight closer to the intended target line.

The most common flaw in this frame is to have the club shaft closer to or aligned with your left arm, as seen in photo 119. This is the "over-the-top" position that you have likely heard of but perhaps never understood. The shaft comes down into impact over the top of the plane of the right forearm, and for most players, this error causes a wild slice or a dead-left pull, depending on the position of the clubface at impact. Either one makes it difficult to hit the ball to your intended target.

Let me make one point about the over-the-top position: you can play great golf with a slight defect. For years I've watched Bruce Lietzke make a very nice living with an over-the-top golf swing. In order to do so, however, you need to make a number of adjustments. First and most important, you have to play with an open clubface. When the shaft of the club swings over the top, the ball will be pulled to the inside of the target line. So if the shot is to have a positive outcome, the ball must curve back to the target line. In Bruce's case, his golf ball starts to the left of the target line and curves to the right. Having done this time and time again, he knows that so long as he keeps the face of the club open, he'll play good golf. Chances are, you don't have the time to practice as much as Bruce Lietzke, so you should aim to correct the over-the-top motion rather than play with it.

So what is acceptable in this position? Basically, as long as the club shaft moves beneath your right shoulder around the right bicep, the shot will be playable. When the club shaft comes down through your right shoulder and into your left forearm, bad shots occur. Your divots get bigger, your shot dispersion increases, ball contact becomes poor, and your scores go way up.

One other thing I want to address is the clubhead's relation to the shaft plane line. There is much debate as to whether the club should be on the plane line in this frame. I would like to see the clubhead on the plane as early as possible, but it is not a necessity. I've seen many good players put the clubhead on the plane line at a later stage than this. Further, if the club shaft is in line with your right forearm, the clubhead will be on or under the plane line, depending on the amount of angle retention between the club shaft and your left arm. So the point to take away from this frame is to work hard at getting the shaft of the club in line with your right forearm. Do this, and you will be well on your way to playing good golf. I believe this is one of the most important frames in the swing because it predicts what will occur when impact arrives.

SWING POSITION 7: PRE-IMPACT

FACE-ON (**PHOTO 120**)

Just as the previous frame in the down-the-line view is an extremely important predictor of impact, this face-on frame provides a telltale snapshot of clubhead speed, ball flight, and something I call "gain."

In case you've never heard it described this way, gain is the difference between the width of the arc in the backswing versus the width of the arc in the downswing. It's measured by first drawing a line at the edge of the clubhead, perpendicular to the ground, when the club shaft is parallel to the ground in the backswing (**PHOTO 121**). Then draw the same line (at the edge of the clubhead, perpendicular to the ground) when the club shaft is parallel to the ground in the downswing (**PHOTO 122**). The distance between the two lines is gain. Players who hit the ball a long way have a large amount of gain, and those who don't hit the ball very

far have a small amount of gain. The more gain you have, the more potential distance you will create.

I also look at the left hand in this frame (photo 122 again). When it first reaches the right thigh, the club shaft should be nearly parallel to the ground. Further, the left arm should be straight and in line with the right leg. You should be able to draw a straight line from the left shoulder through the left arm and down to the right foot. This position is a result of the amount of rotation that has occurred in the upper and lower body as well as the angle retention between the left arm and club shaft.

When your body rotation slows, your arms and hands have to work harder. This makes it very challenging to maintain power and width in this frame and throughout the rest of the swing. As a result, with a slower body rotation you will see in the video that the shaft of the club appears to be drooping as if there were a weight hanging off the club-head (**PHOTO 123**). The shaft is bowing down—this is what happens to the shaft when it is unloading (i.e., losing power). You want that unloading to occur after the ball is hit, not before.

123

SWING POSITION 7: PRE-IMPACT

DOWN THE LINE (PHOTO 124)

Ideally, I would like to see the clubhead slightly under the shaft plane in this frame (**PHOTO 125**). If you're going to hit a draw, the club must come from an inside path. The only way to deliver the club from this inside "power" path to the ball is to have the clubhead under the plane line. This is the greatest struggle for most players, because the desire to get the clubhead under the golf ball in order to lift it into the air, combined with the hit impulse, causes them to swing the clubhead over the top, or above the shaft plane line. The majority of players that I teach slice the ball, and when I look at their swings on video, their clubhead is never on or underneath the shaft plane as it should be.

Another point of emphasis in this frame is that the club shaft should be parallel to the target line. You are once again looking for the short shaft, meaning that from the down-the-line view, the club

shaft will appear virtually nonexistent or very short. When the shaft is both parallel to the ground and parallel to the target line, the camera will show a short shaft. If the shaft in this frame is angled to the right (**PHOTO 126**), then that is the direction the golf ball will initially take. The opposite will be true if the shaft is angled to the left (**PHOTO 127**).

Also note that the right heel should be off the ground and your weight should be transferring to the inside of your left foot (photo 125). Your knee line should be fairly open, so that you can see your left leg outside of your right leg. Your hips should be opening as well, but your shoulders should still be slightly closed to the target line.

Finally, you must pay attention to the clubface in this frame. If you have a square clubface, the toe of the club will be straight over the heel. Most poor ball strikers battle an open clubface, and this frame will reveal it clearly. An open clubface will show the toe of the golf club dragging behind the heel, as if the clubface were pointed more toward the

126

127

sky (**PHOTO 128**). A closed clubface position will have the toe forward of the heel, as if the clubface were pointed to the ground (**PHOTO 129**).

While a square clubface is the goal, I would much rather see the clubface in a closed position than an open one for the average player, and there are a host of reasons why. Golf, as I said earlier in the book, is about energy transfer and collision. In the context of a car accident, there is little doubt that the most severe collision is a head-on one. This is because in a head-on collision, the energy transfer is linear. It is the same concept in golf—the most powerful impact is a head-on (or square) collision. If your clubface is open at the point of collision (impact), then the clubface makes contact on the inside of the golf ball, causing a deflection toward the toe of the club. The open position also adds loft to the clubface. As a result of the increased loft and lower energy transfer, the ball will travel a shorter distance.

When the clubface is in a closed position, the opposite is true. Contact is made toward the outside of the golf ball, causing a slight deflection toward the heel. Also, there is less loft on the clubface, meaning the ball will go farther. When you combine the closed clubface with an inside hit on the golf ball, the result is a nice draw with good distance. This is a shot most golfers would love to hit.

SWING POSITION 8: IMPACT

FACE-ON (PHOTO 130)

This is what your entire swing works for—a picture-perfect impact position. You have now arrived at the moment of truth. As I am sure you can imagine, I have studied this position for hours on end. Without taking away from the value of all that I have discussed so far, in terms of its importance to your improvement, this is *the frame.* Impact is the point where the golf ball is given information and responds. It is the direct result of all the previous motions made in your backswing and downswing to this point. This position is also the most consistent among the best players. No matter what their mechanics look like before this frame, there are a large number of similarities at impact among players with such disparate swings as Tiger Woods, Jim Furyk, and Sergio Garcia.

Analyze this position through the video camera from the ground up as we have been doing throughout this book. First, your left foot should be firmly planted while your right foot should roll onto its instep, with your right heel off the ground. You will notice in photo 130 that my right heel is slightly off the ground and my weight is clearly to my right instep. The left leg is straightening, which is what hitting into a firm left side is all about. The right leg will respond in kind, depending on the manner in which your hips move. If your hip rotation is fairly level, your right leg will not have a lot of knee flex. If your hips are not level as they move through impact, then you will see excessive knee flex (**PHOTO 131**). You will notice how different the lower body looks in these two impact positions. It is clear that the more active the lower body, the less efficient the swing.

It is important to remember that there is the ideal and there is the acceptable. I would not be overly concerned with the position of your right leg as long as your hips have rotated open properly and are level.

You do not want to see your hips remain square to the target line. If they do, your lower body will look very awkward, with excessive knee flex in both legs, and your upper body will hang back. I am not going to discuss the exact amount of rotation, because it will vary for each individual, but the optimal lower-body motion we want to see here is the rotation of the hips into a straightened left leg.

Your upper body should be open as well, so that your chest is facing a point two to four feet in front of the golf ball. Your spine should have a slight tilt away from the target. Again, each individual is different, so the degree of spine tilt will vary, but you want to guard against having so much that you begin to fall back away from the target. Here's a good guideline for spine tilt: your right shoulder should be lower than your left shoulder but still inside your right foot, as shown in photo 130.

One other point to note is the position of your arms. Your left arm should be straight, while your right arm should have a bit of bend in the elbow. The amount of tilt at impact will have a direct effect on the amount of bend in your right elbow, and if there is too much bend, your shoulders and upper body have tilted too much. If you are unable to detect the slight bend, it may appear as a softness in the right arm.

However, the most important element of this frame—and the one true constant among all top players—is the relationship of the shaft of the club to the ball. This face-on view highlights what the best players do at impact. What is most apparent is that the club shaft has a forward lean at impact. The amount of forward lean will vary depending on the length of the club used—while the difference between the 9-iron and the 8-iron will not be too noticeable, it will be very noticeable between the 9-iron and the driver. Since the ball position is farther forward with the driver, the club shaft will have less of a forward lean than it does with a 9-iron. The aspect of impact that does not change from club to club is the relationship of the shaft to your left hip; the shaft should point to your left hip at impact.

Further, as you can see clearly in photo 130, there is a straight line from the left shoulder through the left arm and down to the clubhead. This is where the impact technique of the amateur most differs from that of the Tour professional. It is my belief that because of the instinct to assist the ball into the air, the average player generally has the club shaft pointing toward the center or right side of their body at impact rather than at the left hip, making it impossible to have a straight line from the left shoulder through to the clubhead. When that happens, the club shaft actually leans backward at impact (**PHOTO 132**), causing inconsistent contact because the clubface cannot strike the ball flush when the club shaft leans back. You may also see your left arm bent at impact when the shaft is in a poor position. This photo doesn't show that, but clearly there is more weight on the right side than on the left side.

Some players manage to have the club shaft leaning forward and yet still pointing to the center of their body rather than their left hip (**PHOTO 133**). This can mean that the player has the ball position too far

back or that their body has become too active and has slid toward the target. If this is what you see when you look at your swing on video, know that you may be able to play good golf from this position, but your distance will be negatively affected. My suggestion to you is to use the drills described in chapter five, which can help you find the correct impact position no matter what your fault is. As I mentioned earlier, this is the most important position of the golf swing aside from address. You can never have too much impact practice, and the drills will assist you.

SWING POSITION 8: IMPACT

DOWN THE LINE (**PHOTO 134**)

Impact is the moment when the club should be moving the fastest. When your body is in the wrong position, the speed of your golf club is inhibited. When you freeze your swing in this frame, you should draw three lines: a shaft plane line, a butt line, and a spine-angle line. I will explain how to use those lines later in this section. First look at your right heel; it should be off the ground. How much off the ground will vary depending on the type of shot, the club selection, and your flexibility. I would not get overly concerned with the amount so long as your right knee has not moved dramatically toward the ball. The more knee movement, the more the right heel will be off the ground.

The next element you should look at is the position of your hips. Most great ball strikers keep their hips open at impact so you can see both cheeks of the rear end. Their hips are in this position because their bodies have rotated through the hitting area, carrying their arms and the golf club along for the ride. When you use the arms too much, you won't be able to see your left cheek at impact from this down-the-line view. It will appear as though your hips and body are square to the golf ball, rather than rotating open toward the target. This is a move that steals power from the swing. Also, because your hips will push out toward the golf ball, your spine angle will become more perpendicular and cause your chest to back away from the ball so that your upper body can counterbalance your lower body. If your lower body works toward the ball, your upper body has to work away from the ball in order to maintain balance. Further, when your lower body pushes out toward the ball, the space you have to swing the club through impact has decreased. So if your chest doesn't move up and away, the club will impact the ground well before the ball, defeating the entire purpose of the game. As you can see, an incorrect motion in your hips can cause some serious problems at impact for a number of reasons. When you push your hips out, you have to raise your chest for both balance and space, and the problem becomes timing the contact between the clubface and the golf ball while balancing your body. Remember, the club is moving very fast, and if you attempt to time this contact, you will fail.

Let's return to more positive reinforcement in this down-the-line view of impact. You can see that my right arm has blocked my left arm and there is space between my arms and my body. Both my chest and lower body are open to the target line, which will allow for a complete release, as you'll see in a later frame.

The down-the-line view affords a clear picture of how the club shaft rises at impact. When you examine the impact photo, you can see that my club shaft is almost in the same position it was in at address. Many players raise the club shaft during impact. Again, I want to emphasize that there is an acceptable range and that this is not something to concern yourself with, provided your rear end is still on the same line it was on at address and your chest has not risen out of the shot. If your spine angle has changed, the position of your rear end will shift, raising the club shaft to a level where consistent contact is not probable. The cure for this error is to work on keeping your spine angle constant throughout the swing. In the drills section of chapter five, you'll find an exercise that will assist with this problem.

Finally, your upper body, and specifically your shoulders, should be slightly open to the target line. It should not be nearly as open as the hips, but the openness should still be apparent. If you have maintained the spine angle and tilt you had at address, your chest should be facing toward the ground, as in photo 134.

SWING POSITION 9: POST IMPACT

FACE-ON (**PHOTO 135**)

You have surely heard the term "release" as it pertains to the golf swing, and this is the position where you can see it most clearly. Here are the basics on the release. The golf club should appear as if it is pulling your arms through. Both of your forearms will have rotated, so your left hand will be visible—you can see the fingers of my left hand beneath my right hand in photo 135. If your forearms have not rotated sufficiently and have come through impact stiff rather than loose, you won't be able to see your left hand under the right. Further, improper rotation of the forearms will separate your left elbow from the side of your body—this is called a "chicken wing" (**PHOTO 136**). You can see the left hand above the right hand, and it appears as if I'm pulling the club toward me. This will result in the cupping of the left wrist, which is also apparent in photo 136.

136

137

The final indicator of improper forearm rotation is the right arm. Here in the poor post-impact position you can see the bend in the right elbow. Contrast that with the image of the correct post-impact position, where you see a straight right arm (**PHOTO 137**). In the fault photo, the elbow is bent because of the separation of the left bicep from the left side of the body. When the left bicep separates from the body, the forearms cannot rotate because the left elbow raises up toward the sky. With the left elbow moving in this fashion, a tremendous strain is put on the wrist, creating the appearance of a pulling motion. What is really happening is that the body is fighting with the speed of the club-head, and as a result, the hands are too close to the body, making this position look uncomfortable and forced. The towel drill highlighted in the drills section of the book will assist you with the proper release and force the left elbow to fold correctly.

Additionally, a balance problem will more than likely be evident. When your balance is bad, you will see poor footwork, particularly with your left foot. There are numerous examples of bad footwork, so it is easier to simply tell you what good footwork looks like. Photo 137 again shows you what you want to see: the left heel planted at the post-impact position and the weight on the outside of the left foot. Depending on the amount of flare that you set in your left foot at address, you may even see the sole of the shoe beneath your toes in this frame. This is because your weight will have moved to your left heel, and as a result, your foot will twist and reveal the sole of the shoe. Additionally, your right heel should be to the target side of the toes. If the heel of your right foot is not closer to the target than your toes, you have too much weight on your toes through impact. When this happens, the heel of your left foot will lift off the ground. You will be forced to replant your left foot and move your heel away from the target, making your foot more flared. If you notice this happening in your swing, you are likely changing your spine angle, with your hips pushing out toward the ball.

SWING POSITION 9: POST IMPACT

DOWN THE LINE (**PHOTO 138**)

The first element to look for in this frame is the position of your right knee. Ideally, it will be inside your toe line. Many players who struggle with consistent ball contact have their right knee over their toe line at the post-impact position. If the video of your swing reveals this fault, the rotation of both your upper and lower body slowed at impact and created a possible balance problem as a result of an attempt to assist the ball into the air. At this frame, the movement of weight in your right foot should shift to your instep, which will keep your right knee inside your toe line. This does not mean that your heel should remain on the ground; it just means that you should move your weight to the instep while still allowing your heel to come off the ground. You can see that my right heel is well off the ground while my right knee is inside the toe line.

You should see both your hips and shoulders facing toward the target, with your left hip still touching the butt line I have shown in earlier frames (**PHOTO 139**). Most important, your body should hide your arms and the golf club from view. If you are able to see either your arms or the club, you have cupped your wrists through impact, likely because of the instinct to assist the golf ball into the air. This cupping can also be caused by slowing your body through impact, resulting in a flipping of the wrists in an effort to hit the ball.

If you notice this occurring when you analyze this frame, I suggest hitting golf balls with an overall slower arm speed than usual, with special focus on hitting the ball low. When you hit the ball low, your

body will have to move slightly faster, thereby eliminating the flipping of your wrists through impact.

The final element you should note in this down-the-line view is your spine angle. Have you maintained it into the post-impact position? If you draw a line from your right ear straight down to the ground, it should be to the ball side of your toe line, with your right shoulder significantly lower than your left shoulder (**PHOTO 140**). You will further notice that the left shoulder is slightly below the top of the head. The body has rotated correctly and is facing toward the target. There has been no effort to lift the ball into the air, and the body is still in the correct posture. The incorrect position will show the left shoulder well below the top of the head, because the spine angle has risen and the body has become taller after impact. In fact, the body has stopped rotating and is facing where the ball was originally at address.

140

141

SWING POSITION 10: RE-HINGING OF THE GOLF CLUB

FACE-ON (PHOTO 141)

It is important to understand the effect the shot type will have on the position of your arms, your hands, and most important, the release of the golf club. Regardless of whether the shot is a draw or a fade, your upper and lower body should have roughly the same positioning in this view. Your left leg should be straight, or at least straightening, with both your hips and your chest turning to face the target. Your left forearm should be parallel to the ground and your left hand should be visible beneath your right forearm.

I would not suggest experimenting with different release types (draw and fade) unless your game is to the point where you are a scratch player.

Even then, I would make sure your swing is consistently producing similar shot shapes. Whether it's a draw or a fade, make sure you are producing the same general ball flight with each shot before you endeavor to curve the ball in the opposite direction. There are many different ways to release the golf club, and the manner in which you do it depends on the type of shot you are hitting.

If you're going to draw or hook the golf ball, your forearms should cross, with your left hand visible beneath your right forearm and the forearms almost touching (**PHOTO 142**). You can see here that the release of the forearms has produced a closed clubface, which will draw or hook the ball. The closed clubface is more visible in the down-

142

the-line view, but what's particularly evident from this angle is the rotation of the forearms. The rotation visible in photo 141 is the type of release I'm looking for from the average player. The reason for this goes back to an earlier point: the predominant ball flight of the average player is a slice, which is primarily the result of not rotating the forearms through the impact area but rather trying to assist the golf ball into the air.

Another very important point is the position of the head. Many players have been told to keep their head down for as long as possible during the swing. This is some of the worst advice out there; it could not be further from the reality of what happens in the swing. Your head should be looking up, with your eyes beginning to watch the flight of the ball. If you keep your head down too long, you will delay your body's rotation. This decrease in rotational speed will make your hands overactive—that's the flipping of the hands and wrists that we discussed earlier. Further, if your head does not release properly through the shot, your shots will likely become inconsistent in both distance and direction. The left forearm should rotate counterclockwise so the left elbow is pointing to the ground and the head and eyes are released toward the target. Joe Durant and Annika Sorenstam are two players who have an early head release. These are two of the best ball strikers on the PGA and the LPGA tours, and it is not a coincidence. Keeping your head down through impact impedes your body's rotation and the release of the golf club, and your ball striking will suffer for it. If you are struggling with proper release, I suggest working on the pistol drill and the towel drill, which are illustrated in chapter five.

143

SWING POSITION 10: RE-HINGING OF THE GOLF CLUB

DOWN THE LINE (PHOTO 143)

The key to this frame, and one element you should be looking at, is the exiting of the golf club from your body. In an ideal situation, the shaft of the club should be parallel to its original shaft plane. From the camera's down-the-line view, you should see the club shaft appear to exit between your left shoulder and rib cage. Again, depending on the shot you're hitting, the angle of the club shaft and clubface will change, but your body position should be the same. The release I am showing here is a straight release with the club just slightly closed. Further, your body should be facing the target, with both your upper and lower body having opened completely.

Your left shoulder should be below the level of your head, and your shoulder line should be on an angle that is nearly parallel to the original shaft plane. Again, the type of shot you are hitting will have an effect on your shoulder plane and the angle of the club shaft. The angle of your upper body should still be the same as it was at address. It is a must to maintain your spine angle, and in this frame you should still be aware of it.

144

SWING POSITION 11: THE FINISH

FACE-ON (**PHOTO 144**)

What I like to see in the finish position is complete balance on your left leg. The left leg should be straight so that your hips can face the target. Your right foot should be perpendicular to the ground, with the vast majority of your weight on your left leg. Whatever weight there is on the right foot should be on the toe. You should almost be able to lift the right leg off the ground.

One key to this balance is the position of your right shoulder and your hips. Your right shoulder should be over your left foot and closer to the target than your left shoulder. This position will rotate your shoulders beyond perpendicular to the target, so that the shoulders have rotated further than the hips. In addition, your upper body and hips should be over your left foot. If either your shoulders or hips are not over your left foot, then you have too much weight hanging back on your right leg, which will cause inconsistent ball contact and overactivity in the hands. If you are not balanced correctly here, the step-through drill in chapter five will assist you.

Finally, note the position of the golf club in this frame. I like to have the club shaft pointing to the video camera or the target side of the video camera. This will force you to follow through completely, and will assist with achieving proper balance.

SWING POSITION 11: THE FINISH

DOWN THE LINE (**PHOTO 145**)

One factor I want you to be aware of here is the visibility of the right foot. You can see in the frame that the bottom of the right foot is completely visible, and the foot itself is balanced on the right toe. This view further shows the complete shift of weight onto the left side. There is no falling away from the target, and the weight has properly shifted to the left.

Two additional points to be aware of are the club shaft and the spine angle. You will notice the club shaft has finished around the body and is bisecting the head or neck area. It is not perpendicular to the ground! It is actually somewhat parallel to the shoulder line and close to perpendicular to the spine. The head of the golf club is lower than the hands and closer to the target line than the right foot.

Finally, you will notice that the spine is a little taller than it was at address. This is what will allow your body to have balance. You should allow the body to release completely so you are standing a little taller.

FINAL NOTES

What you will find when analyzing your swing is that, yes, you have flaws. The fact is that every player has flaws in their golf swing. You need to determine if the flaw is affecting the flight of the golf ball or preventing you from getting better. Remember that the purpose of the game is to get the ball in the hole in as few shots as possible. A consistent swing will enable that to happen.

This chapter of the book is very detailed and will require some rereading in parts. It is meant to represent the ideal positioning of the ideal golf swing. Please keep in mind, however, that there are positions in your golf swing that do not have to be perfect, but simply acceptable. I encourage you to use the video camera to assist you with improving your swing. I use the video camera in all my lessons, and I believe it is the only way for you to properly teach yourself. Ultimately, what is important is the golf ball and the flight it takes. Is it consistent? Is it repeatable? Everything is repeatable with practice, hard work, and belief in the swing changes you are making. Remember: you must always know why you are making swing changes and how the ball flight will be affected by them. There is no need to be intimidated. You affect the golf ball; don't let the golf ball affect you!

CHAPTER FIVE

Practice and Drills

I have had numerous conversations with my students regarding how to practice, when to practice, and what to practice. Remember, I am not going to be with you while you practice. In fact, the purpose of this book is for you to learn how to teach yourself. You are going to be the sole monitor of your practice time, and you need to learn a few tough lessons about what's going to happen to you while you practice.

First, there is a good chance you are going to lose focus at some point. You will have a hard time making something click, and so the natural tendency is to begin working on something else. The vast majority of amateurs begin a practice session with one intent and end up working on something completely different. Don't let this happen to your practice regimen. You need to build good habits that will last, and those habits take time to create. If you begin to work on an aspect of your game that has not yet become a habit and then abandon it to address some other matter, you will have wasted your time. The whole purpose of practice is to develop and train a habit. Go to the practice tee with a goal in mind. That goal should be the same every time you practice, until it becomes natural and you don't have to think about it before doing it.

You will also face this challenge: the video camera is mesmerizing. You can see so many things to work on at once that it can become easy to lose focus. I warn you: stay focused! You have to be diligent. If you need to keep a journal and write down what you're working on, then do so. After you devote some practice sessions to working on a particular aspect of your swing, and you are confident it has become a habit, you can move forward and address the next problem. Don't rush it. There is no way to know how long it will take you to ingrain a habit, and everyone's learning curve is different. Here's my suggestion: after two weeks of working on one element of your swing, make an honest determination of whether it has become ingrained or not. If you notice your ball flight changing and you think you've worked on the problem long enough, go get the video camera, set it up in the exact same spot, and see if you've truly improved. It will likely take longer to develop the habit, but I suggest checking after two weeks so that you don't get frustrated and lose focus. Two weeks should be enough time for at least four practice sessions (two per week, ideally). After that, you should see some progress.

You've probably heard of "paralysis by analysis," and this phrase is very applicable to golf. The paralysis is actually caused not by the analysis but by having so many thoughts floating in your mind when you're on the course. Playing with a cluttered mind is the absolute worst way to play the game, because you won't be able to focus on all the elements that make it an actual game.

This overload of swing thoughts is caused by a failure to develop good habits, by a lack of patience, and by rushing the outcome to get to the finish line. Earlier in the book, I made an analogy to walking. You learned to walk long ago, and I am certain that at this point in your life you don't think about how to put one foot in front of the other. You just do it, because it is a habit. The motion of walking is analogous to the motion of golf—when you learned to walk, you learned how to shift your weight both side-to-side and forward-and-back. You learned how to use your arms to assist with balance, and yet you don't think of that now. You just walk. While you may think about the tempo or the pace of your walking from time to time, there is otherwise not much thought involved. In fact, you are likely thinking about other things going on in your life and not really paying attention to the length of your gait. The same should be true of your golf swing. You want to reach a point on the golf course where you are thinking about the types of shots needed to advance the ball toward your target, not the technique you'll use to get it done.

I will also warn you that the way we live our lives in the twenty-first century will likely tempt you to rush the process. You will want your golf swing to be fixed in a short period of time. Remember, you can't rush this. The golf swing is not a fast-food restaurant. You can't order it at one window and pick it up at the next. There is no telling how long it will take, so I suggest you enjoy the process of learning and discovery. Devote yourself to the right kind of practice, and you'll enjoy a better outcome. Further, by committing your practice to creating one habit at a time, you will actually improve faster.

Before I discuss the drills that will help you improve, I want to address the purpose of practice and its benefits. Any understanding of how to analyze your swing using video is useless without proper practice. I see it all the time—a student will take a lesson, and then, two weeks or so later, I'll see that student working on something totally different from what we discussed in the lesson. Upon inquiry, I'm usually told that the student read about or watched something and thought they would need to work on that rather than on what we had talked about in our lesson. In effect, they have gone backward.

Training a good habit takes time, and that is especially true if the motion is vastly different from what you have been doing. Until it is habit, you should address it and work on it through practice. So the object is to create good habits—I cannot emphasize this enough. You want to avoid too much thinking when you're hitting the golf ball.

On his way to victory at the 1997 Masters, Tiger Woods established three records. He was the youngest player ever to win the Masters, at age twenty-one; he set the lowest winning score, 270; and he won by a record number of shots—twelve. To win by twelve shots in any tournament is fantastic, but to do that in a major championship is staggering. Yet with all that success, Tiger decided to change his golf swing. He and his then–swing coach, Butch Harmon, went about reworking his swing so that, among other things, he could square his clubface at the top of the swing. Tiger had played with a closed clubface, which made controlling his distance, especially with short irons, difficult.

The point to the story is that it took almost eighteen months before Tiger's game returned to the level he was accustomed to. This is the best athlete to ever play the game. Tiger is in great shape, and he's one of the hardest working athletes in any sport. And still, it took him a year and a half. Making changes in your golf swing will take time, and you have to be patient with the process.

The first step in that process is to learn how to practice effectively. Always give yourself *at least* two weeks to make one change in your swing. When you are working on a swing change, you will need to alter the way you practice so that you spend at least half the practice session repeating a drill that will help you ingrain the change. If possible, alternate from the drill to the full swing and back to the drill. This will help you learn the feel of how to correct the flaw. So spend the first half of the practice session on the drill only, and then alternate between the drill and the full swing in the second half. At this point, don't worry about where the ball goes, because you are only working on one element in the swing. There will be plenty of time to worry about the golf ball when you start to work on impact, but at this point, thinking about that will only be a hindrance. Remember, you are solving a problem one step at a time. Solve the problem. Solve . . . the . . . problem! You'll solve the problem by focusing on it and it alone. This kind of discipline will help you improve at a faster rate.

There are so many drills in golf, but I'm going to include only the ones that I feel will assist you in the different aspects of the swing. I prefer to characterize them by the description of what is being performed. Those descriptions and the pictures provided will help you perform them correctly. I emphasize that you should not rush the development. It takes time, and you may need more or less time than another player does.

Practice drills are a very important part of improvement. They are a necessity in achieving a sound and consistent golf swing. It is obvious that the golf swing is a learned behavior, and a number of key elements must be mastered in order to build a fundamentally sound swing. I believe that everyone can master the movements of the swing, and repetition through the use of drills will allow that to happen. What I further believe is that you must focus on one element at a time, which is why each of these drills has a specific purpose that corrects a problem. If you become impatient and try to solve all your problems at once, you will only lead yourself to the land of confusion. You won't improve by having multiple thoughts about your swing at one time. It's impossible to play consistently good golf that way, and it's inefficient to practice that way.

I would like you to use each drill for the purpose of solving a problem. The drill may not lower your score immediately; however, that does not mean it's not working. In fact, you may find that you struggle with ball contact when you begin to make a change. This happens because when you make a change, your hand-eye coordination is not adept enough to contact the golf ball solidly. I am not saying you will definitely face this situation, but you might, and I don't want you to be discouraged as a result. I often explain to students that if they are able to make contact with poor mechanics, imagine how much better they will become when they are able to improve those mechanics. The point is that you must be diligent in maintaining a single thought until it is mastered, and that may take some time.

The use of the video camera will assist you in determining whether you have mastered the desired swing change, and I suggest you use the camera to verify your success. While you may feel that your swing is changing, the video will confirm whether this assumption is true. I rarely go to the practice tee without the video camera. I would suggest having your camera with you at all times, including during the following drills. Bringing it to the practice tee is as important as bringing your golf clubs!

ONE-ARM BACKSWING DRILL

- **PROBLEM:** You see on video that your club is not on plane.
- **PURPOSE:** To get your arms and body working together correctly.
- **PROCEDURE:** Use a mid-iron. Take your right hand off the golf club at address (**PHOTO 146**), then make a backswing (**PHOTO 147**). Pause at the top and place your right hand back in its original position on the club (**PHOTO 148**). The key is to now swing the club into impact without searching for extra distance. Avoid placing your right hand on the golf club and then swinging even farther back. Additionally, you don't want to pump the club to start the downswing. This is not a drill that should be performed quickly.

    When you place your right hand back on the club, make sure your grip is correct. It's okay if you have to look at the grip to confirm that you are placing your hand on the club correctly. Take your time! Again, you are trying to teach yourself what it feels like to stop the club in the correct position. Drills are designed to assist you with developing the proper feel. Don't be preoccupied with the outcome of the shot.

This drill offers a number of benefits. It will help you groove a better backswing, because your arms and body will stop together. You are making a one-armed backswing, so you won't be as strong. As a result, your body and your arms will work together. Your left arm will truly "lead" the swing, keeping the club more in front of you. You can

see that the backswing in this drill is shorter than normal. This is fine because what you are trying to do is feel the club on the proper plane. Depending on your flexibility, your arm will tend to stop when it has reached about shoulder height. You will notice a natural rotation of your left forearm when making a one-armed backswing. This important element is often misunderstood. You will want to remember this forearm rotation when you return to a conventional swing.

Finally, this drill slows your tempo down—something most of us can use. With only one hand on the club, you will move the club more slowly. This slower movement, combined with the pause at the top of your backswing, makes this drill an ideal fix for an overly quick swing tempo.

CLUBFACE-IN-THE-MIRROR DRILL

- **PROBLEM:** Your clubface is misaligned at the top of the backswing.
- **PURPOSE:** To learn what a square clubface looks and feels like.
- **PROCEDURE:** First, set up with the right side of your body facing the mirror. Make a full backswing and check the angle of the clubface in the mirror. Ideally, the clubface will be parallel to your left forearm. You should repeat this drill as often as possible. Lean a golf club in front of a mirror in your home, and check the position of the clubface every time you use the mirror. If you can make a commitment to doing this, you will quickly establish a feel for the correct position.

As I mentioned before, the clubface is the most important element in controlling the direction and flight of the golf ball. You must ensure that the clubface is in a square position, and the one place where you can monitor that easily is at the top of your backswing.

This drill also emphasizes a key point: the more you can see what you are doing with your golf swing, the better you will become. When you can't use the video camera, the mirror is the best substitute. It will be very valuable for checking posture, ball position, and other parts of the swing. Though it isn't as effective as the video camera, the mirror is a great teaching tool. You can rely on it as you continue to use practice drills.

HIP DRILL #1: POINT LEFT FOOT TO TARGET (PENGUIN DRILL)

- **PROBLEM:** You have too much lower body movement in the backswing.
- **PURPOSE:** To create the proper motion sequence between upper and lower body.
- **PROCEDURE:** The left-foot-to-target drill is also called the penguin drill. I like this drill because it addresses two faults: it restricts lower body movement in your backswing and assists with the opening of your hips and torso at impact. Here's how to perform the drill: Take your normal stance, and then open your left foot so it is pointing at the target (**PHOTO 149**). The foot should be positioned parallel to

the target line, creating a natural restriction of your hips during the backswing. Your knee bends toward your toes, so when your foot is pointed out, your knee movement is limited. In fact, your left knee will stay outside of your left hip throughout the drill. This position will enable you to make a controlled backswing, and that is the reason many top players open their left foot at address. If you have a problem with an overactive lower body during the backswing, especially extra movement in your knees and hips, this drill will solve it.

One of the biggest uncertainties facing all golfers is using their lower body correctly. Simply put, your lower body reacts to the movement of your upper body in your backswing. Nothing in this game is simple, however. You have to teach yourself a number of elements in the golf swing, and sometimes you have to teach yourself *not* to do something. That's the case with this drill, which helps you stop overusing the lower body in your backswing and avoid poor weight distribution.

One note of caution: this drill is difficult if you have limited flexibility. I do not want you to injure yourself, so if you have a problem with flexibility, perform this drill with only half- or three-quarter-length golf swings. Ideally, you'll be able to point your left foot directly at the target (parallel to the target line). However, not everyone is that flexible, and pointing it at a sixty- or seventy-degree angle will still allow you to get the desired benefit from the drill.

HIP DRILL #2: WEIGHT ON OUTSIDE OF FEET (JOHN WAYNE DRILL)

- **PROBLEM:** You have too much lower body movement in the backswing.
- **PURPOSE:** To create the proper motion sequence between upper and lower body.

- **PROCEDURE:** The idea here is to place as much of your weight as possible on the outsides of your feet (**PHOTO 150**). When you do this correctly, your knees remain over the feet rather than over the insteps. Now make a swing, and be sure to keep your weight on the outsides of your feet during the complete motion. You will feel the restriction of the hips and the torque of the upper body. This is a drill you can incorporate into your actual golf swing.

With both this and the previous drill, you will feel a restriction of your hips and a limit to the extent they can turn in the backswing. Your hips will remain level through the motion, allowing your upper body to rotate properly over a stable lower body. Try both of these drills and see which one works better for you.

150

PATH DRILL: ROLL THE DICE

- **PROBLEM:** An improper swing path.
- **PURPOSE:** To visualize an improved swing path by using instant feedback.
- **PROCEDURE:** Place the tees in the ground in a pattern like the dots on the five side of a die (**PHOTO 151**). Set the forward tees one club-head apart, and do the same with the trail tees. The total distance from front to back or left to right should be about six or seven inches. The four corner tees should be at least two inches tall— don't sink them completely into the ground, or they won't show if you've performed the drill properly. I've numbered the tees from 1 to 5 to make things easier to understand.

Place the golf ball on tee number 3, which is in the middle. Let's say your video analysis has revealed that you swing too much from outside to in across the target line. When you use this drill to work on swing-

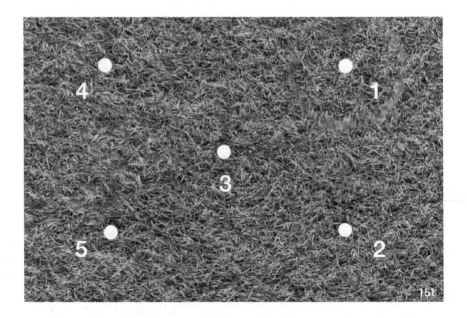

ing the club more from in to out, you should contact tees 2, 3, and 4 (**PHOTO 152**). When you do this drill correctly, only tees 1 and 5 will remain undisturbed.

Conversely, if you are working on delivering the club from outside to in, you should contact tees 1, 3, and 5 (**PHOTO 153**), with tees 2 and 4 remaining undisturbed. Make sure to focus your attention on the tees and not on the golf ball. In fact, you can do this drill without a golf

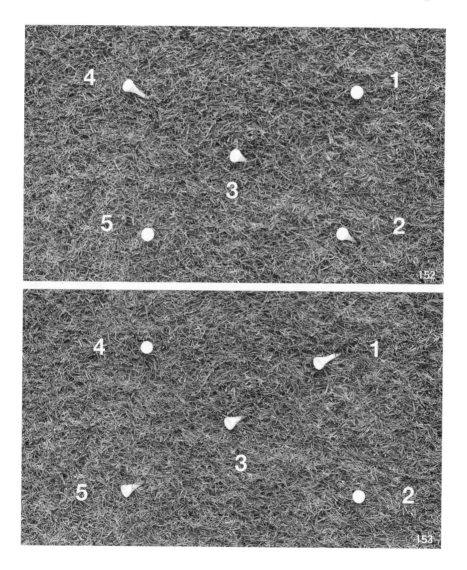

ball. I recommend that you start with half swings at half speed. As you begin to get a sense of how the correction feels, increase the length of your swing but not the speed. Once you have become more comfortable, slowly start to work up to full swings at full speed. This drill is all about teaching yourself the correct feel, and slowing your swing down will assist with the learning curve.

As I said earlier in the book, the two factors that control the direction of the golf ball are the clubface and the path of the club. This drill is designed to work on your feel for the path. Regardless of your skill level, you should gain a basic understanding of how to control the path of your club. Ultimately, players who struggle with the path either swing too much from out to in or too much from in to out.

I recommend this drill for everyone. It's very simple, and requires nothing more than tees. You might use golf balls or head covers in other drills that help you correct a flawed swing path. However, I prefer using just the tees, because they provide a visual advantage and deliver instant feedback.

You should be aware that you are probably swinging along the path where you would contact tees 1, 3, and 5. The most common mistake among amateur golfers, this error will produce either a pull or, more likely, a slice. To make the ball draw or hook, you must swing the club along a path that contacts tees 2, 3, and 4. Now, understand the golf ball will not draw until the clubface is in a closed position at impact, but you cannot hit a draw unless the path of the club is contacting tees 2, 3, and 4. When you hit those tees, you will notice that the ball is starting more to the right. I emphasize *starting* to the right because it may continue to go farther right. But if it's starting to the right, you are performing the drill correctly.

I mentioned earlier that the clubface needs to be closed at impact in order for the ball to draw. However, this drill is about initial ball flight and delivering the club into the ball on a correct path. If the ball isn't curving the way you want it to even when you're consistently hitting the tees you desire, that is a clubface issue, which can be worked on in the clubface-in-the-mirror drill or the towel drill.

BUMP-THE-WALL DRILL

- **PROBLEM:** You come up out of your posture during the swing.
- **PURPOSE:** To train yourself to hold the correct spine angle from start to finish.
- **PROCEDURE:** This drill is impossible to perform with a golf club, because you will likely hit the wall. So don't even try—you will do some very bad things to yourself, your house, and your golf club if you do! Take your normal address position in a place where you can push your rear end up against a wall with your arms across your chest (**PHOTO 154**). Make the motion of a backswing and maintain the connection of the wall with your right butt cheek (**PHOTO 155**). When you begin the downswing, place your left butt cheek back on the wall. Swing down through impact and into your follow-through, keeping your left butt cheek against the wall. As you get to the follow-through, the wall should be touching your left hip (**PHOTO 156**).

This drill is designed to teach you how to maintain your spine angle through the entire swing. As I mentioned before, the movement of your spine angle during the swing is a common problem that can cause tremendous inconsistency. This drill will teach you what it feels like to maintain your spine angle from start to finish.

This drill also demonstrates the proper rotation of your hips, which is what changes the point of contact with the wall from your right butt cheek to your left butt cheek to your left hip. You want to perform this drill slowly so you can feel how your body weight is transferred from side to side and from toe to heel. Creating consistency with your spine angle will create consistency with your ball flight. This is one of the biggest amateur faults I see, and this drill will assist players of all ability levels.

154

155

156

PISTOL DRILL

- **PROBLEM:** You have poor hand action in the downswing.
- **PURPOSE:** To prevent the overuse of your hands.
- **PROCEDURE:** First, take your normal grip and stance. Then lift the thumb and index finger of your right hand off the club (**PHOTO 157**). Make sure that when you look down at the grip, you see your right thumb and index finger on the right side of the grip (**PHOTO 158**). Your right palm should be pointing directly at the target. When you hold the club correctly with this drill, you'll be able to see the part of the grip where your right thumb and forefinger were, and also the thumb of your left hand. This is one of the best all-around drills for any player because it is designed to help you maintain your wrist angle, or lag, in the downswing and also helps with grip pressure, tempo, and a free release of the club.

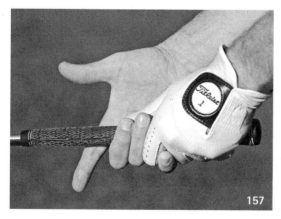

157

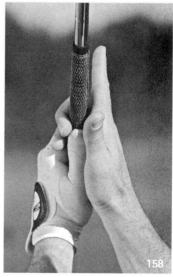

158

When you first try this drill, it is tempting to allow your right thumb and index finger (the ones you took off the club) to curl over the grip (**PHOTO 159**) either at the start of or during the swing. Make sure you don't fall into this trap, or the drill won't do what it is designed to do. After you have hit the ball, bring your arms and hands back in front of your body to check that your right thumb and index finger did not curl over the club during the swing.

As you practice with this modified grip, you should feel as if you have limited control over the club. That is the exact idea. You want the club to lag in the downswing, which means that your hands lead the clubhead into impact. Removing your right thumb and index finger from the club limits your control, and you can focus on the delay between the backswing and the downswing. It will feel like you are loading the club shaft and delaying the hit, which is what all good players do. I am confident that after you repeat this drill a few times and get used to the grip, you will be surprised at how well you can hit the ball and how far it will go with limited effort.

As an aside, I want to tell you a story relating to this drill. I was just beginning as an instructor at the Dorset Field Club in Dorset, Vermont, and one of my female students was having a difficult time with her swing. She was pulling all of her shots, and no matter what she thought about or what I told her to do, she continued to pull the ball. She had a very sound golf swing, and this problem aside, she was a very talented player. However, she just could not get rid of "the pulls." After a number of lessons, I asked her to do the pistol drill. About twenty minutes later, she began to strike the ball very solidly, and most important, she no longer pulled her shots. Extremely encouraged, she left the practice tee with a sense of accomplishment. The next day she had the same success on the practice tee. However, out on the golf course, she quickly returned to pulling the ball. Now very distraught, she expressed her frustration to me. We scheduled a lesson for the next day, and I watched her perform the pistol drill to perfection.

This is the way things went for almost a month, until one day when things changed. She went out to the golf course and experienced the same success she had found on the practice tee. Thrilled with her achievement, she came out to find me on the practice tee and let me know of her improvement. Later that summer, she won the ladies' club championship.

I tell you this story because it is important to understand that the length of time needed to achieve a swing change is unpredictable, but with patience and perseverance, you will accomplish your goal. Making changes in our behavior, whether in our golf swing or in everyday life, isn't easy. But you must trust that what you are working on will have positive results.

TOWEL DRILL

- **PROBLEM:** An incorrect release of the club through impact (i.e., a chicken wing).
- **PURPOSE:** To develop proper forearm rotation and release the club.
- **PROCEDURE:** Place a towel in the armpit of your left arm (**PHOTO 160**). You'll have to apply some pressure with your arm to keep the towel lodged in your armpit while you swing the club. Take small practice swings at first to develop an understanding of what this feels like.

When you introduce the golf ball into the drill, make half swings at half speed. You are not attempting to hit the ball far; you are learning how to rotate your left arm through impact—and well past it, in fact. In order for your left arm to fold properly into the finish, your left elbow must point toward the ground after impact (**PHOTO 161**). The proper rotation of your left forearm allows your left elbow to fold correctly. In the frame, you can see the left hand and forearm beneath the right hand and forearm. This is a position I'm sure you rarely experience. I don't recommend making full swings with this drill; doing so will greatly inhibit your freedom in the backswing and will discourage forearm rotation when you move the club away from the ball. This drill is strictly for one purpose: training the proper rotation of your left arm through and after impact.

160

161

STEP-THROUGH DRILL

- **PROBLEM:** A reverse weight shift through impact and into the follow-through.
- **PURPOSE:** To teach your body to feel the correct weight shift.
- **PROCEDURE:** Begin with your feet close together (**PHOTO 162**). When you bring the club back to start the swing, your right foot should lift and take a step back with the club (**PHOTO 163**). This will teach you to shift your weight to your right side. When the club nears the top of the backswing, your right foot should be firmly planted on the ground, and you should lift your left foot off the ground. Then, as you begin the downswing, step forward and replant your left foot as you swing toward the target (**PHOTOS 164, 165, 166, 167, AND 168**). Your body should move through impact, allowing your right foot to again lift off the ground and walk through toward the target as you swing to the finish (**PHOTO 169**). When you perform this drill enough times, you will emerge with a feel for how to properly transfer your weight.

The step-through drill helps you conquer one of the biggest challenges you will face as a golfer—achieving the proper weight shift. The most common weight-shift problem is a reverse weight shift, in which your weight moves forward in the backswing and backward in the downswing. This type of motion usually results in very poor contact and a weak slice. Further, your divot (if you make one) will point dramatically to the left of the target. I have seen a variety of poor shots hit from a reverse weight shift, and I must say it is the most common cause of a lack of distance and inconsistent performance.

Video footage from the face-on angle will show you that in a reverse weight shift, your head and body are moving forward (toward the target) as you swing the club back. Many times you will see your head dip down toward the ground. On the downswing, your body moves away from the target and possibly lifts up from the ground. It is as if your body is moving like a seesaw—precisely the motion you don't want. The step-through drill will make it impossible to perform a reverse weight shift. By shifting your weight to your right and lifting your left foot along with the weight shift, you will learn the feel of a proper weight shift into the right side. After working with the step-through drill, go back to filming your swing. You will notice that your head remains level and your weight loads onto your right foot on the backswing. This loading motion will allow you to shift your weight toward the target during the downswing, thereby eliminating the reverse weight shift.

162

163

166

167

164

165

168

169

BALANCE DRILL

- **PROBLEM:** An inability to master good balance through the golf swing.
- **PURPOSE:** To determine the proper pace and rhythm to your swing.
- **PROCEDURE:** This drill is not complicated, though it is actually more challenging than you might think. Simply hit the golf ball and hold your finish until the ball comes to a complete stop.

The balance drill has a number of benefits. Every swing needs balance to succeed, and this drill is an easy and effective approach to fixing balance problems. It will also teach you not to overswing. You will find there is a speed at which you can swing the club and not lose balance. Incorporating this drill into your practice will help you determine that speed. Your tempo will improve very quickly. Finally, the drill will teach you the proper rhythm for your golf swing. Do this drill at the beginning and the end of your practice sessions on a regular basis.

LAG DRILL FOR BETTER IMPACT

- **PROBLEM:** Lack of distance on full-swing shots.
- **PURPOSE:** To create maximum clubhead speed at impact.
- **PROCEDURE:** Begin this drill using your pitching wedge, making half swings at half tempo. Increase the length of your swing but don't change the tempo until you can make a full-length swing and achieve the objective of the drill.

Tee the ball up just above the level of the grass and place a second ball about eight to ten inches behind the ball you're hitting (**PHOTOS 170 AND 171**). Always tee the forward ball up when you're working on this drill—it will take more time but it is much more productive. Place the rear ball just slightly to the inside of the target line. The object is to hit the forward ball without hitting the rear ball. It sounds easy, and may be easy as you make half swings to begin with. It will become more challenging as your swing increases in length and speed.

Once you've improved to the point where you never hit the rear ball, move it closer to the forward ball you are hitting. The optimal space between the balls is five to six inches. Be careful of the angle of attack, which is the angle at which the club comes down to impact. Some of my students actually create a steeper angle of attack when doing this drill, which is something to avoid. You will know you are doing this if your divots begin to get too large and too deep. A steeper angle of attack may help you avoid the rear ball, but it won't improve your lag or impact position.

In fact, lag is one of the hardest elements to teach in the golf swing. I usually teach this after my student has developed their motion and has a solid hold on the basic concepts of the swing. Lag requires tremendous feel in your arms and wrists, so I would urge you to wait until your game is at the point where you are playing consistently. This drill is designed to add distance to your game and improve your impact

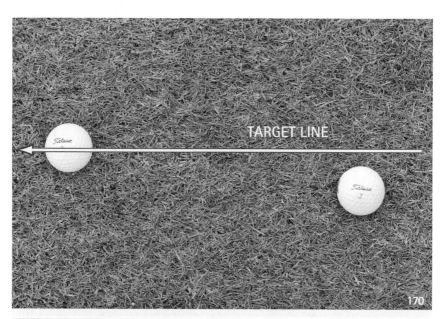

position. It is one of the most difficult drills, and you should monitor yourself with the video camera to make sure you are doing it correctly, especially at first.

To monitor this with the camera, use the face-on angle. The shaft of the golf club should be pointing to your left hip at impact, as in photo 27 (on page 14). When you perform the drill correctly, you'll notice this forward lean in the shaft. Further, you should record both the drill and your regular full swing, without the rear ball. You will see a big difference between the two impact positions at first. In time, you will notice improvement in both your impact position and your distance.

The feel you are looking for is softness in your arms and wrists. You should feel your wrists are setting even more in the downswing. You may even feel a whipping motion occur, and if you do, that's terrific. You want to create and store energy until the last possible moment before impact. That is the essence of lag.

With this drill, you will notice a change in your ball flight. It will become lower and more piercing in its trajectory. You will also notice that the ball has more backspin, particularly with your wedges. So pay attention to what the ball is doing when it lands on the green.

BOX DRILL

- **PROBLEM:** Poor impact position and weak contact.
- **PURPOSE:** To create a more powerful impact (a better collision).
- **PROCEDURE:** This drill requires a box about five feet long and four to six inches wide. The best boxes to use, in fact, are those in which club manufacturers ship golf clubs. Check around your garage to see if you have empty boxes, or ask your local PGA club professional if he or she has any extra golf club boxes.

Place the box on the ground so that the long end is parallel to the target line (**PHOTO 172**), then slowly impact the box and attempt to drive it forward (**PHOTO 173**). Your aim here is to move the box forward without having it rotate (**PHOTO 174**). Any rotation that does

172

occur should be in a counterclockwise direction (**PHOTO 175**), which will indicate that you are swinging from the inside-to-out power path—the path needed to produce a draw or hook. The box will move in a clockwise fashion only if you swing across the target line from out to in, which will produce a fade or slice (**PHOTO 176**). If you see that clockwise rotation, you know you're making a mistake.

This drill illustrates a simple but important point: golf is a game of collision. It is a collision between the clubhead and the golf ball. For the best possible collision, you need to swing the club along the ground (horizontally) rather than into the ground (vertically). When the collision is delivered more horizontally than vertically, the energy transfer from club to ball will be at its maximum.

Do the box drill for at least two weeks (you may need to get a few boxes), and you will change the way your golf club impacts the ball. You should feel a more solid strike and notice much greater distance.

CHAPTER SUMMARY

- Making a significant change in your golf swing will take more time than you might expect. Be patient and stick with your practice routine until you develop a good habit.
- Don't become preoccupied with ball flight when making a change in your swing. You should be working on only one element at a time, which will help you develop the proper feel.
- Use the video camera to monitor your progress as you practice.

CHAPTER SIX

Now What?

You are almost at the end of the book. Now what do you do with all this information? It is my hope that you better understand how to analyze your own golf swing and that you know how to practice so your improvement is all but assured. No doubt, there is a lot of advice to comprehend and absorb. So what should you do now?

Well, I have some thoughts. First, remember what I told you in the beginning of the book about setup and its importance in creating a consistently good golf swing. Prior to looking at your swing on video, you need to make sure that your grip, posture, body alignment, and ball position are correct. Your swing is a reflection of your setup, and if those mechanics are poor, chances are your swing will reflect that. So make certain you begin your effort by correcting any flaws in your pre-swing. Only then should you move on to analyzing your golf swing.

I also suggest that you practice with positioning the camera properly and make sure you are recording your swing from consistently correct vantage points. Getting used to the camera will take some time, and you should become proficient with its operation before analyzing your swing. If you position the camera incorrectly, you may begin fixing something that doesn't need fixing. Therefore, I would suggest you take the camera out a couple of times and simply record your golf swing to be sure the camera is positioned properly. If you want to take a look at your swing, that's fine; however, do not begin to evaluate your swing or start to fix anything. It may not need fixing. In fact, whether it does is irrelevant, because at this point you are simply learning how to use the camera, not fixing your golf swing. So learn to use the camera. Spend time with it. Understand that the camera is the key. If you don't have the proper familiarity with the instrument, all the recordings of your golf swing will be meaningless. You have to know where to position the camera, how to record properly, and all the other information detailed in the first chapter of this book. Get comfortable with the camera so when it comes time to record your swing for real, you will be prepared.

This book has armed you with enough information to be your own swing coach. Now you have to use the information constructively. This is a very challenging task that can be thought of in this way: When you build a house properly, you must make sure the foundation is established and is strong. Once the foundation is built, you can progress to the framing and a host of other tasks that must be done to ensure the home is properly built. You don't put the roof on before the house is framed, because it simply won't work.

The golf swing is no different. You have to understand cause and effect and know that some flaws affect others. By solving one problem, you may be solving two or three. But by skipping steps and going right to the "roof," you will create new problems. Therefore, you must start with the setup and then work on the backswing, downswing, impact, and so on. If you work on impact without working on the backswing, you will lose your way, because a fault in your backswing may be hindering your ability to achieve the correct impact position. This is cause and effect.

I have focused this book on the entire golf swing and how to analyze it properly, from the backswing to the follow-through. You need an understanding of the complete motion, because all of its parts are related. Every part of the golf swing has an effect on what is to follow. If your backswing is unorthodox, the remainder of your swing must counterbalance it. The point is to take one step at a time and progress in the correct order. When you do this, you will have success in teaching yourself a better golf swing.

So how do you know when your swing is ready for the next step? The answer is that you have to record your swing and work on your drills during practice so that you ingrain good habits. That way, your mind can be free of swing thoughts and will create the right motion. If you've been working on your backswing and now want to see if your work has created a good habit, you have to empty your mind of swing thoughts. I suggest making repeated swings where all you focus on is tempo. You might even consider taking your iPod with you to the practice tee and listening to music while you practice. The point is to distract your mind from swing thoughts so that you can focus solely on tempo. By concentrating on tempo and not technique, you will be free of your backswing thoughts. Then check your swing on video for any change. If the change is better but not exactly what you are looking for, you are not ready to move on to the next step. Continue to work on your backswing until you have made the progress you desire and are not forced to think about it. Develop your habits through practice, and focus on just one element at a time. That is the best way to improve your golf swing.

There is one other bit of information I'd like to impart. I warn all of my students to use caution when reading instruction articles in magazines, watching the Golf Channel, or listening to whoever is offering advice on the golf swing. These avenues of information have made many players more knowledgeable about and more comfortable with instruction concepts and terminology. The problem is these avenues are providing information that may not apply to what you are working on in your golf swing. And while the information may be useful at some point, it may not be useful at this time in your game.

Again, stick to one thing at a time and stay with the plan. If you do this, I promise you will make the changes necessary to improve your golf swing. If you alter the plan, the chances that your improvement will be derailed go up exponentially. Not everyone wears the same shoe size. Just because a shoe is on sale for a good price does not mean it fits or that it is right for you. If it is the wrong size, you will be wasting your money. Information about the golf swing is the same. It may be good information, but it may not be good for *your* swing. So don't be tempted to find the quick cure. It is not out there. Only practice, patience, and perseverance will lead to real improvement. Good luck, and enjoy the journey!

ACKNOWLEDGMENTS

I would like to thank a number of people who have made this project possible.

First, Judith Curr, my publisher, who listened to an idea and believed in it.

To Nick Simonds, my editor: thanks for your direction.

A special thanks to Greg Midland, without whom this would never have happened. Greg, you have allowed me to fulfill a dream, and I am extremely grateful.

To my family—Pop, Mom, Giff, Alan, and Becky—I could never have asked for better.

To Uncle Peter Fleming: thanks, Pos, for your wisdom.

Thanks to Ted Kiegiel, who is a brother in every sense of the word.

To Tom Kochan, who showed me the importance of being a golf professional: thanks, Doc.

To Will Fleming, Tom Henderson, and Mike Summa—you guys have been a valuable resource in assisting with the book. Thanks for taking the time.

To Darrell Kestner: thanks for teaching me how to teach. You have always shared your ideas about the golf swing, and I am grateful to have worked for you.

Special thanks to Jim Schmid. You and your staff at the World Golf Village could not have been more accommodating.

A heartfelt thank-you to photographer Sam Greenwood and Cheryl Carnegie. Your tireless hours are truly appreciated.

Thanks to all the golf professionals who have directly and indirectly influenced my life. Knowledge is something gained and passed along. I am fortunate to be in the middle of it all.

ABOUT THE AUTHORS

Michael Breed is Head PGA Professional at Sunningdale Country Club in Scarsdale, New York. He was named the 2000 Metropolitan Section PGA Teacher of the Year, was given the Metropolitan Section Horton Smith Award in 2006 and 2007, and is one of *Golf Magazine*'s Top 100 Teachers. He lives in Greenwich, Connecticut.

Greg Midland is an author and the editor of *The Met Golfer*, the official publication of the Metropolitan Golf Association.